Educating Literacy Teachers Online

Tools, Techniques, and Transformations

LANE W. CLARKE
SUSAN WATTS-TAFFE

Foreword by Julie Coiro

TEACHERS
COLLEGE
PRESS

Teachers College, Columbia University
New York and London

Published by Teachers College Press, 1234 Amsterdam Avenue, New York, NY 10027

Library of Congress Cataloging-in-Publication Data

Clarke, Lane W.
  Educating literacy teachers online : tools, techniques, and transformations / Lane W. Clarke, Susan Watts-Taffe.
      pages cm
  ISBN 978-0-8077-5496-2 (pbk. : alk. paper) —
  ISBN 978-0-8077-7249-2 (e-book)
      1. Language arts teachers—Training of—United States. 2. Literacy—Study and teaching—United States. 3. Language arts teachers—Training of—Technological innovations. 4. Language arts teachers—Training of—Computer-assisted instruction. 5. Teachers—Training of—United States. I. Title.
  LB1576.C5625 2014
  372.6′044—dc23   2013034036

   ISBN 978-0-8077-5496-2 (paper)
   eISBN 978-0-8077-7249-2

Printed on acid-free paper
Manufactured in the United States of America

21 20 19 18 17 16 15 14   8 7 6 5 4 3 2 1

LANGUAGE AND LITERACY SERIES

Dorothy S. Strickland, FOUNDING EDITOR
Celia Genishi and Donna E. Alvermann, SERIES EDITORS

ADVISORY BOARD: Richard Allington, Kathryn Au, Bernice Cullinan, Colette Daiute, Anne Haas Dyson, Carole Edelsky, Shirley Brice Heath, Connie Juel, Susan Lytle, Timothy Shanahan

(continued)

For volumes in the NCRLL Collection (edited by JoBeth Allen and Donna E. Alvermann) and the Practitioners Bookshelf Series (edited by Celia Genishi and Donna E. Alvermann), as well as a complete list of titles in this series, please visit www.tcpress.com.

To my husband, Brock, and sons, Quinn and Ambrose, who have understood my need to be tethered to my computer, which often meant working until late at night and on weekends—thank you for your understanding and support.

—*Lane Clarke*

To my husband, Dennis, and to my children, Jonathan and David— thank you for your love, joy, and encouragement throughout this project.

—*Susan Watts-Taffe*

Contents

Foreword

For several years, I have considered teaching one of my college courses in a completely online format. Online learning experiences offer the flexibility to accommodate multiple schedules, they can broaden the range of individuals within a learning community, and they can provide immediate access to a range of interesting people and digital resources. Ironically, although my research focuses on online reading comprehension and inquiry, multiple concerns and a few personal fears have kept me from making the transition to online instruction. I have lingering questions: How will I be able to personally connect with my students when I can't even see them? How can I model important literacy practices, and watch as my students experiment with these practices, when we're not even in the same room? Will my online courses have the potential to match in-class learning outcomes? How will I intervene outside of my face-to-face office hours when my students don't understand the content or need extra help? And the most frightening question, perhaps: How will I know how to actually teach well in such complex online spaces? More often than not, when I thought about these questions, the answers pushed me just a little too far out of my comfort zone and I'd decide to put off my course design for a later time.

However, this book has truly changed all of that. In their book, Lane Clarke and Susan Watts-Taffe explain, in friendly language, why and how to design online course experiences that can be engaging and personalized without sacrificing quality and rigor. Firsthand words of wisdom from other experienced online instructors, activities to try, and literacy-specific online assignments woven into each chapter offer concrete examples of how to successfully design an online literacy course for literacy educators. The authors' intentional focus on the instructor rather than the technology at each point in the course design process reassures me that online and hybrid experiences can still reflect socio-constructivist theories of learning and effective teaching practices, albeit re-envisioned through the lens of new digital tools and spaces. Put simply, Lane and Susan have inspired me to be a little braver and take the plunge into online course design.

Today, literacy educators are under enormous pressure to address rigorous standards in reading, writing, listening, and speaking while customizing their instruction to meet the needs and concerns of all students. We also live in a time when things change quickly. As Lane and Susan point out, the nature of learning, teaching, teacher education, and literacy is rapidly changing in ways we can no longer ignore. Effective literacy teachers need to continually revisit and update their thinking and practices to reflect these changes. Similarly, professional development experiences should be preparing our pre-service teachers to skillfully employ digital tools and build personal and professional networks for their literacy lives after college. This book effectively lays out general guidelines and specific techniques for how to model these important skills by engaging our literacy teachers in the digital practices we hope they will employ in their own literacy classrooms. In addition, each author's reflections about her personal journey toward re-envisioning courses as a set of online learning experiences shed light on the process of redefining our own identities as online teachers of literacy teachers.

Readers may be interested to know that this book grew out of conversations that began in a series of study group meetings, first at the university level, and then with a larger group of educators at two annual meetings of the Literacy Research Association. The meetings were designed to bring forth and support genuine concerns of literacy teacher educators grappling with how to capitalize on the affordances of new technologies while still building the specialized knowledge and expertise required to develop strong readers and writers in schools. As such, this book meets educators where they are, validating concerns that the process of moving courses online is time consuming, requires multiple levels of technical support, and demands new ways of thinking about how to best meet accreditation requirements. And yet one cannot help but be convinced that the extra time and effort is well spent. As you read, be prepared to experience a compelling journey through underlying principles of effective professional development, practical examples of how online and hybrid learning experiences benefit both learners and teachers, and instructional models that have been used successfully to strengthen critical learning outcomes for reading professionals. This might very well be the book that inspires you, like me, to find a trusted colleague, take a few risks, and begin your own journey toward moving a literacy course or whole program online.

—Julie Coiro, PhD
associate professor
School of Education
University of Rhode Island

Acknowledgments

When I started teaching online I thought that it would be a solitary endeavor—just me and my computer. I was pleasantly surprised at how wrong I was! Teaching online has proved not just to be collaborative but also transformative; it has changed how I think about the teaching and learning process and my identity as a teacher. I have many people to thank who have supported my thinking, learning, and practice. First, I want to extend a huge thank you to Susan Watts-Taffe. I am so grateful that our initial monthly lunches not only inspired many wonderful conversations, but also supported a study group, research, and now this book! As Susan and I initially wrestled with issues of online teaching, we were fortunate to have the support of a Literacy Research Association Study Group focused on educating literacy teachers online. For a number of years we engaged with wonderful participants who got up at the crack of dawn and collaboratively shared ideas and challenged one another to think more deeply about online education. Some of these study group members have been generous enough to contribute their voices to this book, specifically Marianne McTavish and Kenneth Weiss. In addition, Erica Boling gave us excellent feedback on our initial idea for this book. I have also been fortunate to have a wonderful team of adjunct instructors at the University of New England, who have gone above and beyond what they are paid to do and contributed to offering wonderful literacy courses—they are my amazing team—Karen Deterding, Courtney Graffius, Linda Lacasse, and Peggy Wallace. When I started teaching in the online master's program our director, Greg Kearsley, was integral in ensuring my success. His modeling and encouragement were instrumental in my confidence as an online designer, teacher, and researcher. My colleague Audrey Bartholomew helps me chart new directions and areas of research, and Tony Hanson and Aaron Brady provide countless measures of technical support.

—Lane Clarke

For me, learning to teach online is an ongoing journey. I am grateful to my colleague and friend, Lane Clarke, not only for making this a shared journey but also for the vision and tenacity needed to bring this book into being. Throughout my exploration of online teaching, I have learned a great deal from Lane, as well as from my colleagues at the University of Cincinnati: Suzanne Ehrlich, Allison Breit-Smith, Holly Johnson, Cheri Williams, Connie Kendall Theado, Chet Laine, Ying Guo, Heather Neal, Kathy Hoover, and Sarah Schroeder. I am particularly grateful to my on-line students, from whom I continually learn what works, what doesn't, and what more is possible. My commitment to their learning is inspired by their commitment to *their* students' learning.

—Susan Watts-Taffe

Finally, we are grateful to our editorial team at Teachers College Press, especially Emily Spangler and John Bylander, for diligently working with us throughout this endeavor.

—Lane and Susan

Educating
Literacy Teachers
Online

VOICES FROM THE FIELD

Although the challenges in designing and teaching an online course are many, they are exciting and continue to shift my thinking. I keep reshaping content and delivery in my quest for good pedagogy and increased student engagement. In some ways this can be both frustrating and exhilarating. My first challenge is to make the course "come alive" in a virtual context. I can easily develop and maintain this in a face-to-face context through the physical mode—the gestures, the gaze, the proximity—which leads to the feeling of a shared space and the sense of a collective. I find that building a virtual classroom community can be done, but it needs to be carefully constructed. I am able to gain support from our technology department to present course content digitally (e.g., voice-over Power Points, podcasts, wikis, and prezis) and provide assignments that can be completed in interactive ways (e.g., VoiceThread, discussion boards, chat rooms, and blogs). I am having some success. The preparation work for the course and teaching the course have been very time consuming, but I am finding satisfaction in attending to multimodal instruction and to the various learning styles of my students.

—Marianne McTavish,
Department of Language & Literacy Education,
University of British Columbia, Vancouver

The digital age we are in should be changing how we educate students into a more engaging, interactive, and personalized experience. Yet teachers currently practicing and students pursuing graduate teaching degrees are unlikely to have much experience using digital learning in the classroom with their students. Modeling this through instructor-created material allows teachers to have firsthand experience with how material can be tailored to a particular audience as they consume it. When teacher work submissions capitalize on digital creation, it allows them to have practice in the field. In turn, they are more equipped to use digital learning with their own students.

—Courtney Graffius,
adjunct graduate instructor, University of New England,
technology integrator, Scarborough Public Schools, Maine

Introduction

Questions to Ponder

- How do you see inservice teacher education and professional training changing?
- What do you believe is most challenging about online teaching and learning?
- What do you believe is most promising about online teaching and learning?

The idea for this book began at informal monthly lunch meetings. Lane had just started teaching an online course for her university, and Susan was working toward full implementation of an online graduate-level reading endorsement program at her university. Between iced teas and deli sandwiches, we wrestled both with how to translate face-to-face pedagogy into our classes and also with how to take an entire program of study online. These meetings were filled with micro-questions such as the following:

- How do I teach someone how to conduct a reading conference or a miscue analysis online?
- Is there a way for teachers to video themselves? Can they upload these and share them with others?
- How can I model using technology tools that I hope my teachers will use in their own classrooms to enhance *their* students' literacy development?

There were also macro-questions such as these:

- How can I be an effective teacher if I don't actually "see" my students?
- How can I ensure quality and rigor through a program that is not delivered on-site?
- How can we evaluate the effectiveness of an online program of study?
- How do we prepare and support faculty to effectively engage in this new teaching environment?

3

As we confronted these questions, we thought surely there were resources available to support us. We were surprised to find that there were not. Although we did find many helpful books and journals focused on distance education and online pedagogy on a broad scale, we did not find any resources dealing specifically with the questions that are pertinent and unique to educating *literacy teachers* online.

We quickly realized that our monthly meetings provided a critical support, and we imagined that other literacy teacher educators wrestled with similar micro and macro questions, either with their colleagues or alone. This led us to facilitate a study group focused on the topic of online literacy teacher education at two of the annual meetings of the Literacy Research Association. Our conversations with literacy education faculty from different regions of the United States and Canada confirmed that a book such as this would be useful. This need was reaffirmed at the 2011 Preconference Institute of the International Reading Association (IRA) focused on the preparation of reading professionals, where participants expressed questions and concerns related to meeting the IRA *Standards for Reading Professionals* (IRA, 2010) in online programs.

In light of our own explorations and the new directions in teaching afforded by 21st-century information and communication technologies, we designed this book to focus on inservice teacher education and development in literacy, including its specialized theoretical knowledge, requirement for applied expertise, and associated disposition for working directly with readers and writers in schools. This book comes at a time when many factors are shaping literacy education in new and significant ways. First, computers and the Internet are drastically changing the way we consume, interact with, and produce knowledge; in effect, the very nature of learning has undergone a tremendous shift in the last 20 years. This dramatic shift can be both stimulating and mind-boggling. While technology integration makes sense in today's digital world, we must carefully consider how we carry it out. When we explore technology as a set of tools to promote active, constructive, and social learning in our online environments, we maximize our effectiveness as literacy teacher educators. Second, teacher education and professional development have been in the spotlight for the past decade, with particular attention focused on the national debate on how to improve students' literacy achievement and close the "achievement gap." Palloff and Pratt (2007) assert that "standards for learning are now higher than they have ever been before, as citizens and workers need greater knowledge and skill to survive and succeed. Education is increasingly important to the success of individuals and nations" (p. 2). Determining the best ways to support teacher effectiveness has been at the center of this conversation. Simultaneously, the very definition of literacy is changing to accommodate the landscape of 21st-century skills. Digital literacies are integrated throughout the Common Core State Standards (CCSS) for English Language Arts and Literacy in History/Social Studies, Science, and Technical Subjects, with references to digital reading and writing as early as grade 2 (National Governors Association Center for Best Practices & Council of Chief State School Officers, 2010). Online literacy teacher education lies at the nexus of these movements, and yet very little attention has been given to actively shaping it in ways that increase and enhance teacher learning and, ultimately, improve student learning in K–12 settings.

THE CHANGING FACE OF TEACHING AND LEARNING

There is no denying that online graduate programs in education are on the rise. The number of universities and colleges that offer online master's degrees in education is staggering. According to *USA Today* (Toppo & Schnaars, 2012), online degrees in education have skyrocketed, with the top four degree-granting institutions in education being online. Further, according to the U.S. Department of Education, 1 in 11 postgraduate degrees in education are granted by online programs (Toppo & Schnaars, 2012). Teachers are turning to online programs of study for a variety of reasons. Getting a master's degree online, once a novelty, is now commonplace and readily accepted by school districts. Many teachers seek a master's degree to move from the classroom into more specialized areas and administration. Many states require a master's degree after a certain number of years in the classroom, and this graduate degree is often linked to a salary increase. For a variety of reasons, teachers are drawn to online programs, as they offer the flexibility and convenience that fit into their busy lives.

The increase in online enrollment in teacher education mirrors a larger trend in online education. According to the Sloan Consortium report (2011) *Going the Distance: Online Education in the United States, 2011*, 6 million higher education students—almost one-third of all students in higher education—are taking at least one online course. The rate of growth in online education is ten times higher than it is in the overall higher education population, and the projections for growth continue to rise. Palloff and Pratt (2007) believe that "online education is in its infancy, with far more change to come in the not too distant future" (p. xx).

The explosion in online education has also led to a change in the demographics of specific courses and programs of study. Courses that may have been relatively homogeneous in student makeup now include students from different parts of a single state, different regions of the country, and even different parts of the world, thereby shifting the demographics of our classes. In each of our respective institutions, we've experienced greater racial and ethnic diversity among students in online courses than in our face-to-face courses, including far more teachers in rural American settings who now have access to our programs of study, as well as teachers from international locations.

In addition to the growth in online programs housed in colleges and universities, online professional development opportunities offered within school districts and professional organizations have increased. Increasingly, school districts are utilizing online delivery systems to reach teachers and to cope with constrained budgets. Similarly, professional organizations use online tools to reach record numbers of teachers, especially around topics of national concern such as the CCSS and Response to Intervention. According to Ash (2012), many educational leaders see the development and implementation of online professional development as the key to successful implementation of the CCSS.

The fact that teachers across states and districts can participate together with the same content has significant ramifications for how we envision inservice teacher education. In this vein, many professional organizations are creating online communities, offering webinars, and developing podcasts to reach practicing teachers. For example, both the International Reading Association (IRA) and the National Council of Teachers of English (NCTE) support vibrant online collaborative learning communities and also sponsor periodic webinars on topics that are relevant to literacy.

THE CHANGING FACE OF TEACHER EDUCATION

Recently, teacher education programs have been in the spotlight. In the 2006 report *Educating School Teachers,* Levine called for a transformation in teacher education programs, suggesting that many existing programs inadequately prepare future teachers to make a significant impact on the achievement of their students. Following No Child Left Behind (2001), with its focus on teacher accountability, data-based decisionmaking, and higher standards for student learning, national attention has been given to teacher education through initiatives such as Race to the Top (U.S. Department of Education, 2009) and President Obama's 2011 plan for teacher education reform and improvement (U.S. Department of Education, 2011). Further, in 2010, IRA adopted a new set of *Standards for the Preparation of Reading Professionals*, requiring that reading teachers demonstrate high levels of competence with respect to Foundational Knowledge, Curriculum and Instruction, Assessment and Evaluation, Diversity, Literate Environment, and

Professional Learning and Leadership. With the expectation of increased quality in teacher education, the integrity of online teacher education programs is a paramount concern.

Juxtaposed with this reality is another: A potential expansion of research-based characteristics of effective teacher education/professional development, as supported by the technologies of online teaching and learning. Those who study teacher learning and change over time point to the importance of situated learning, coaching, reflection, inquiry, and communities of practice (Darling-Hammond, 2006). Specifically, it has been argued that new technologies lend themselves to such sociocultural, constructivist approaches to teaching, learning, and literacy (Chandler-Olcott & Lewis, 2010). And, as indicated previously, online teacher education offers greater opportunities for cultural and geographic diversity among teacher participants, which can lead to richer understandings of sociocultural influences on literacy learning. As teachers engage in professional development communities that are not geographically bound, the notion of "communities of practice" changes.

More broadly, many literacy teacher educators are interested in the ways in which sociocultural, constructivist theories of learning are enacted in online learning spaces. Within this context of literacy and learning as social practices, we need to continually redefine how online teaching can do the following:

- Facilitate sociocultural, constructivist practices
- Support and create tools that are most effective
- Determine how to appropriate these tools in ways to promote "meaningful, purpose-driven" (Watts-Taffe & Gwinn, 2007) instruction
- Ensure equity of access in the online learning community

THE CHANGING FACE OF LITERACY

According to Prensky (2001), today's students have morphed into digital-native citizens who are profoundly different from their predecessors (he refers to those individuals as digital immigrants). Prensky used the term *digital native* to describe children who have grown up with technology and thus have a different relationship with it than those who did not grow up in such a technologically saturated world. The Kaiser Foundation surveyed 2,002 3rd–12th-grade students, ages 8–18, and found that current students' time with technology has increased dramatically in 5 years and that these students devote an average of 7 hours and 38 minutes to using entertainment media during a typical day (Rideout, Foehr, & Roberts, 2010).

With respect to literacy in particular, it has been argued that attention to digital literacies in literacy methods courses is way behind the integration of technology and literacy in the K–12 classroom, and that both of these lag terribly behind in recognizing the changing face of literacy beyond the classroom—that is, the literacy demands of a globally engaged citizenry in the 21st century (Leu, 2007). It is clear that new technologies are changing the very nature of what it means to be literate (Leu, Kinzer, Coiro, & Cammack, 2004; Warschauer, 2006) and, by association, the very nature of what it means to be a literacy teacher. In the *Handbook of Research on New Literacies*, Coiro, Knobel, Lankshear, and Leu (2009) suggest that literacy is no longer defined by "the ability to take advantage of the literacy potential inherent in any single, static, technology of literacy . . . but rather by *a larger mindset* and the ability to *continuously adapt* to the new literacies required by the new technologies that rapidly and continuously spread on the Internet" (p. 5, emphasis added). They further posit that "literacy will also include knowing how and when to make wise decisions about which technologies and which forms and functions of literacy most support one's purposes" (p. 5). Chat rooms, blogs, podcasts, wikis, streaming video, and discussion boards are just a few of the new technologies that simultaneously offer new literacy opportunities and require new literacy skills, strategies, dispositions, and social practices. Since new technologies are constantly changing, the ability to "learn and relearn" is an integral part of being literate in the 21st century. This is a vast deviation from the traditional tenets of literacy, which focus on learning a discrete set of skills once and for all. Of critical concern is the decisionmaking required as we use these new technologies as tools for teaching and learning.

Survey data suggest that teachers' use of technology has risen in the last decade, with more resources allocated to teacher professional development in this area than in the past (National Center for Education Statistics [NCES], 2000). Still, there is much to learn about the most effective ways to integrate technology into teaching, specifically as it relates to literacy instruction (Karchmer, Mallette, Kara-Soteriou, & Leu, 2005). Anecdotally, we have not observed that teachers enrolled in online courses necessarily integrate technology into their own work with students in effective ways. Historical research, however, points to the notion that teachers teach as they have been taught. This begs a critical question for those of us engaged in online literacy teacher education: How can we model practices that our students can appropriate in their work with their own students? At a time when learning is changing, teacher education is changing, and literacy is changing, the time has come to focus on developing resources of intellectual support and community for those who are navigating this new terrain.

DEFINING ONLINE AND BLENDED LEARNING ENVIRONMENTS

How we define literacy in this new technological world and how we educate and support teachers online has exploded with wonderful potential learning opportunities. While we will use the term *online learning* throughout this text, it is important to recognize that online learning can encompass a variety of formats. Online teaching and learning can be asynchronous, where interaction is not dependent on time or space. The defining features of completely online experiences are that the teacher and the student do not share a physical proximity and that learning can be done on a flexible schedule determined mostly by the learner (usually within guidelines and time frames established by the teacher). For many, this is the model that they are using and seeing used in their settings. Blended learning, also known as hybrid learning, refers to a combination of face-to-face learning and online learning experiences (Vignare, 2007). Typically, the percentage of time spent online distinguishes a blended instructional model from other models. Proportions vary, with universities and educational agencies having their own specific definitions, but in general a blended learning experience can be compared to other learning experiences as follows, based on Allen, Seaman, and Garrett's (2007) descriptions:

- *Blended.* A blend of online and face-to-face instruction with approximately 25–75% of instruction occurring online, with the important distinction that a percentage of face-to-face learning time is *replaced,* rather than simply augmented or enhanced by online learning time (Caulfield, 2011).
- *Web-Enhanced or Web-Facilitated.* Face-to-face instruction, in which web-based technology is used to enhance or supplement what is done in class (e.g., using a Course Management System to post the syllabus, readings, and announcements that are pertinent to class).

Picciano (2007) noted that blending occurs on a continuum, with great variation in the degree to which face-to-face experiences and online experiences are balanced.

Results of the last national survey of educational experiences in the United States, conducted in 2004, indicated that graduate-level blended learning options were nearly as prevalent as online learning options, with 21.9% of public institutions offering blended courses, compared with 25.9% offering online graduate courses. In the field of education, however, blended learning opportunities exceeded online learning opportunities, with 36.5% of public institutions offering blended courses compared with 24.9% offering online courses (Allen, Seaman, & Garrett, 2007).

This book will use the term *online* throughout to establish some guidelines and ways of thinking about how to construct learning experiences in this unique setting. While Chapters 1–5 do not specifically name blended/hybrid learning, we do feel that all of these chapters are relevant to both settings. In Chapter 6, we will circle back to comparing blended with fully online course designs and discussing specific factors to consider when choosing between a completely asynchronous platform and a blended learning environment. Since the field of education still relies on both formats, it is important that we think about online teaching in a broad sense but also address the intricacies of choosing a balance that aligns with your objectives.

HOW THIS BOOK WILL HELP YOU
NAVIGATE ONLINE TEACHING AND LEARNING

This book is meant to serve as a resource for literacy teacher educators and professional development trainers who teach and work in online settings. Specifically, it is designed to assist professionals in translating general online learning theory to the unique discipline of literacy. This book includes tools and techniques for those engaged with developing courses, workshops, or other online learning experiences (including blended/hybrid delivery formats that combine face-to-face meetings with online experiences). The resources, tools, and templates provided will support instructional quality and rigor, ongoing student assessment, and reflection. In an attempt to create and sustain a collaborative learning community focused on these issues, this book is supplemented by a website (www.educatingliteracyteachersonline.com) through which readers can access regularly updated resources. Additionally, this virtual professional development community for online literacy teacher educators will allow members to communicate and share resources with one another. Finally, this book will encourage those in the field to extend their thinking and enable online literacy teacher education to grow in productive ways. More than simply a "how-to book" for online literacy teacher education, this book is meant to fuel thinking and ongoing conversation in the field.

HOW THIS BOOK IS ORGANIZED

Each of the six chapters begins with questions to ponder, which will activate your thinking about the content of the chapter. We've tried to balance research and theory with practical applications, examples, and sample assignments, and we conclude each chapter with suggestions of activities to try. Between chapters you will find the opinions and perspectives of a variety of online educators reflected in sections that are called Voices from the Field.

Several major themes serve to anchor the book. First, the instructor, rather than the technology, is in the foreground. This is an intentional move away from discussions of online education in which the technology and delivery systems dominate the conversation. We argue that instructors should be concerned, first and foremost, with strong pedagogy that results in student learning. In this, the teacher is central. Second, the purpose of instruction is to promote student learning. Toward this end, instructors need knowledge of an array of new technologies and related tools coupled with guidance in making decisions about which tools to use for which instructional purposes, and how best to maximize the use of selected tools. Third, the rapidity with which new technologies are changing requires a disposition toward future exploration and continued learning. Therefore, instructors need not learn only about current available technologies, but also the strategies and dispositions required to adapt to technologies as they evolve and continually challenge the landscape of what is "new." Fourth, instructors across the country (and internationally) vary considerably in their experiences with and dispositions toward technology use in general, and online teaching and learning specifically. For some, the content of this book will be entirely new, and perhaps somewhat foreign to established ways of thinking and doing. For others, the content will be familiar, to varying degrees. We assume great variation, so the book is designed to meet a variety of readers at a variety of points on their professional journeys, and to provoke further thinking and forward growth for all of us.

The chapter order reflects our anchor themes. The first chapter (Chapter 1: Establishing Our Online Identities) highlights our belief that in any online learning experience the teacher needs to be front and center. The next three chapters (Chapter 2: Building and Sustaining Effective Learning Communities; Chapter 3: Technology Tools That Promote Active, Constructive, and Social Learning; and Chapter 4: Designing Effective Learning Experiences) present effective practices associated with distance education, with specific applications to literacy teacher education. In the final two chapters (Chapter 5: Supporting Critical Learning Outcomes for Reading Professionals and Chapter 6: Changing the Landscape for Reading Professionals Through Online Learning) we foreground literacy teacher education by addressing the professional standards to which our courses are held and the changing environment of teacher professional development, which includes online and blended options.

We wish that we had this book when we were sitting at lunch wrestling with many of the issues that are presented in the coming pages. We hope this text will serve as a life raft for those who need it and also as a launching pad for new ideas and new paths in online literacy teacher education. We see online teaching and learning as a new frontier in helping teachers to improve their literacy instruction and hope this book serves to explore current practice as well as suggest new directions. Thank you for joining us both through this text and also through our online companion site (www.educatingliteracyteachersonline.com) to work together to create effective online educational experiences for literacy teachers.

VOICES FROM THE FIELD

Perhaps more than anything else, my experiences with students in online learning environments have clarified my understanding of and, in turn, deepened my appreciation for creating classrooms that function as communities of practice (Lave & Wenger, 1991; Wenger, 1998). Guided by the premise of learning as social participation, communities of practice bring together the "knowing" and the "doing" of any shared domain of interest, such as, in my case, the knowing and doing of postsecondary literacy education. What I find most compelling about this particular theory of learning for online instruction is its dual focus: the collective pursuit of new understandings through sustained conversation and information-sharing over time and the consequent building of meaningful social relationships among participants and across the virtual classroom landscape. Because students in online classes can sometimes feel a remoteness from one another and the instructor, my ability to provide regular opportunities for students to both learn from and contribute to the classroom community's growing knowledge base becomes all the more important.

Establishing a strong online teaching presence is, I believe, central to this process of creating a virtual community of practice. Different from leading discussions, answering questions, or otherwise guiding students through the curriculum, being "present" as an online teacher requires me to take fuller account of the nuances of classroom discourse, generally, and to embrace my role as co-participant in the educational process, in particular. Since online interactions often take place asynchronously, with the words of students and teachers captured and held separately in the shape of discussion board threads, encouraging the kind of collaborative meaning-making vital to the teaching/learning transaction can be a challenge. In response to this challenge, I have become a more attentive and charitable reader of my students' words and ideas as well as a more reflective and invitational writer myself. In other words, I notice more, ask questions more, check my impressions more, search out connections more, and so engage more completely with my own and my students' meaning-making processes. As a result, I am able to position myself as both teacher and learner and, in so doing, I encourage my students to claim this dual role for themselves: the surest means of becoming a fully fledged community of practice in any classroom environment.

—Connie Kendall Theado, associate professor,
Literacy and Second Language Studies Program, University of Cincinnati

CHAPTER 1

Establishing Our Online Identities

Good teaching cannot be reduced to technique; good teaching comes from the identity and integrity of the teacher.

—Parker Palmer, *The Courage to Teach*

Questions to Ponder

- What do you think makes a good teacher?
- How is teaching online different from teaching face-to-face?
- If you have done both, what do you do differently online from what you do in a face-to-face classroom?
- In what ways has teaching online challenged/enhanced your sense of what it means to be a good teacher?

Identity is inextricably linked to teaching. In a synthesis of research on faculty experiences of teaching online, Major (2010) found that teaching online is accompanied by the deconstruction and reconstruction of faculty personas and stances. In other words, faculty find that "going online" changes their sense of self as instructors. Simultaneously, Richardson (2010) asserts that new technologies demand new thinking about content, curriculum, and the best ways to teach students. Among the "big shifts" he cites are: learning as a "24/7" enterprise; learning as social, collaborative, constructive, and meaningful; and teaching as conversation, not lecture. The degree to which these are big shifts or little shifts depends a great deal upon the way we have historically situated ourselves as teachers with respect to our students, and now, also how we situate ourselves with respect to the technologies of online education.

Leu (2007) has argued for quite some time that literacy teachers and literacy teacher educators have not been centrally engaged in conversations about, and constructions of, the new ways of teaching and learning afforded by new 21st-century technologies. It is because of the primacy of the teacher in the learning process that we begin this book by examining who we are as teachers, including our identities and orientations toward learning. This stance is particularly important in a conversation about online instruction, since there is ongoing concern that online programs are primarily motivated by student demand and profit potential, as opposed to pedagogical considerations (Toppo & Schnaars, 2012). Additionally, much of the language used to discuss online teaching and learning reinforces a secondary role for the instructor. Terms such as *distance learning, course delivery,* and *course design* focus on the course, rather than on the teacher, as the impetus for student learning. And while the term *distance learning* suggests learning as a process as well as an outcome, parallel terms that focus our attention on teaching as a process are not prevalent.

According to Darling-Hammond (2006), teacher quality is among the most important contributors to student achievement. Research has shown that as teachers become more qualified, student achievement rises (Ferguson, 1991). In *What Matters Most: Teaching for America's Future,* the National Commission on Teaching and America's Future (1996) stated, "What teachers know and do is the most important influence on what students learn" (p. 6). The importance of the teacher also transcends to the online world. For example, when universities survey students who drop out of online courses, students often cite lack of "teacher presence" as a major contributing factor (Smith, 2005).

We argue that placing the educator, rather than the technology, at the center is crucial to the success of any online learning experience. However, online learning changes the conceptualization of centering the teacher, especially since learning is no longer bound to the constraints and conventions of physical space and previously held notions of teaching (Saltmarsh & Sutherland-Smith, 2010). Teachers are "being challenged to re-think their underlying assumptions about teaching and learning as they become online educators" (Baran, Correia, & Thompson, 2011, p. 421) and this is complicated by the fact that many of us have not been "trained" to teach online—many of us learn on the job with little or no guidance (Moore & Kearsley, 2012; Smith, 2005). Much of the training available has been focused on the tools and logistics of online teaching, with little or no attention paid to our role in the online learning environment and how this impacts our identities as online teacher educators. As Baran, Correia, and Thompson (2011) assert, a "teacher's role in the online environment is dynamic and multidimensional, requiring a more integrated look at teachers' work through pedagogical problem solving with their disciplines" (p. 434). With respect to the discipline of literacy teacher education, we adhere to social constructivist theory, which asserts that learning is mediated within a social context. As a collaborative experience, it is through interactions with others that we learn new concepts and ways of being (Vygotsky, 1978). From this perspective, knowledge is constructed as individuals engage in activities, receive feedback, and participate in various forms of human interaction (Henning, 2004), and the teacher plays an active role in these dynamic "participatory inquiry-based learning practices" (Baran, Correia, & Thompson, 2011, p. 436). It is our belief in social constructivist learning and the importance of the teacher in this process that leads us to consider how online teaching impacts who we are as teachers.

SITUATING OUR PROFESSIONAL IDENTITIES

As far back as Lane remembers, she has defined herself as a teacher—in her bedroom as a child teaching her stuffed animals to read and write, as a 4th-grade teacher, as a parent, and then as a college professor. This was not just what she did; it was who she was. For many of us, our identities are defined not just by what we do, but also by how that shapes our interactions, outlooks, visions for ourselves, and place in the world. We *are* teachers—and now many of us are teachers of teachers. In teacher education the practice of teaching represents more than content and course delivery, as discussed by Saltmarsh and Sutherland-Smith (2010), who examined how teachers defined themselves as they moved from face-to-face teaching to online teaching. In their study, they investigated how changes in the mode of delivery impacted not just the *"how* of teaching but also the *who* of teaching—the ways in which teaching subjectivities are conceptualized, experienced, and produced by teacher educators" (p.15). Focusing on the *who* of teaching is an important first step as we begin to establish our online teaching identities.

Saltmarsh and Sutherland-Smith (2010) stated that "for a number of teacher educators in our study the move from face-to-face classrooms into online teaching is relatively new and poses considerable challenges to strongly held views and commonplace practices implicated in the production of teacher subjectivities" (p. 20). This transition from a comfortable, known teacher identity to a new identity as an online educator does not require us to throw away what we know, but rather to build upon our existing teacher identities (McCarthey & Moje, 2002; Trevitt & Perera, 2009). Our professional identities are created within the context of established norms and discourses, and our work, as we adjust and redefine ourselves, is to map our new identities onto the foundation of our existing ones. Saltmarsh and Sutherland-Smith (2001) assert that "while teacher educators' subjectivities are undoubtedly shaped by their emerging technological skills and new roles in their workplaces, their approaches to online teaching continue nonetheless to be mapped onto what they see as firmly held professional values and entrenched pedagogic practices" (p. 21).

In the remainder of this chapter, we will explore some of these entrenched pedagogic practices and discourses as we think about how our new identities are mapped onto these current practices, and we will consider both the overlap and the tensions in establishing a new identity as an online educator. Uncovering the discourses that shape our identities as teachers—specifically, as online literacy teacher educators—will empower us to continue to center ourselves as active participants in the online learning environment. First, we consider the discourses of what makes a good literacy teacher and what makes a good college instructor. Then we will connect these beliefs to what makes an effective online educator. Finally, we will explore some tensions that may arise as many of us renegotiate our identities as online educators.

What Makes an Effective Literacy Teacher?

For many of us, our identities are defined not just by what makes a good teacher but by what makes a good teacher of literacy. While the two are often intertwined, researchers have studied specific behaviors that have been linked to positive reading gains in students. For example, Wray, Medwell, Fox, and Poulson (2000) identified several behaviors of teachers whose students make gains in literacy:

- Effective teachers provided high quality of instruction with maximum range of opportunities to learn. They had clear classroom organization and engaged students in a combination of learning arrangements, such as whole class, small groups, and one on one.
- Effective teachers facilitated engagement with tasks that matched with student interest and used a variety of effective teaching skills, such as questioning, modeling, feedback, and adjusting pace.
- Effective teachers were attentive to teacher–pupil interaction.

Michael Pressley spent much of his career researching effective teachers and schools across different settings and over changing periods of time. In addition to many of the aforementioned characteristics, he found that effective literacy teachers diversified the complexity and balance of learning activities, were able to adapt to meet individual needs, made frequent checks on student progress, set high expectations, and encouraged self-regulators who were independent and active thinkers (Mohan, Lundeberg, & Reffitt, 2008).

As Topping and Ferguson (2005) point out, sometimes we are not aware of the instructional practices in which we engage because they have become second nature. One of the benefits of moving our pedagogy online is the opportunity to bring these practices to the surface. Thinking about how to become effective online educators requires critical reflection on our current practice. See Figure 1.1 for a set of questions to ask yourself as you translate good practice online.

Figure 1.1. Prompts for Moving Effective Instructional Practices Online

Effective Teachers of Literacy . . .	Questions to Ask Yourself as You Move These Practices Online
Provide a range of diverse learning opportunities	In what ways do you present a variety of learning opportunities in your online courses?
Establish clear expectations	In what ways do you establish and articulate clear expectations through your course organization and materials?
Create a variety of learning arrangements	How do you engage your students in whole-class, small-group, and one-on-one interactions?
Stimulate engagement	How do you motivate your online students? How do you know if your online students are engaged?
Engage in questioning	What types of questions do you ask? Do they span different levels of complexity?
Model their thinking and best practice	How, and how often, do you provide models of effective practice in your teaching?
Vary pacing of activities	How would you describe the pace of activities in your course? What indicators do you use to determine whether the pace is appropriate?
Encourage teacher-student interaction	How do you encourage your students to interact with you? What types of interactions do you most often engage in with your students?
Monitor student progress through frequent checks	Are there opportunities for frequent checks of student progress throughout the course—both for you and for your students?
Promote independent thinkers	In what ways do you support a growing ability to think independently over time?

What Makes an Effective Literacy Teacher Educator?

For many of us, we first established our professional identities through teaching in K–12 settings. As each of us shifted to the world of academia we needed to map our existing identities onto the discourse and culture of teaching in higher education. Luckily, although the content changes a bit, and the learners are a bit taller, the practice of teaching is not much different. For example, Chickering and Gamson (1987) identified the following seven principles for good instructional practice in higher education:

- encourages interaction between students and faculty
- encourages interaction and collaboration between students
- uses active learning techniques
- gives prompt feedback
- emphasizes time on task

- communicates high expectations
- respects diversity—talents, experience, and ways of learning

Most of these practices are similar to what effective literacy teachers do in their classrooms. In addition, Young and Shaw (1999) surveyed college and university students to better understand how students perceived effective professors. They found that attributes such as being an effective communicator, creating a comfortable learning atmosphere, displaying concern for student learning, motivating students, and communicating clear course organization were most important. Clearly, the primacy of the teacher-student interaction is just as important when educating adult learners as it is with children. Furthermore, delivering content through varied learning opportunities, paying attention to tasks, and pacing instruction were also important. Finally, high expectations, attention to the individual learner, and frequent assessment permeated the culture of what made for effective teachers at both levels. Given these similarities, we imagined that effective online teaching would be characterized by the same set of practices, and that translating these practice for an online environment would be fairly straightforward. However, Dieklemann, Schuster, and Nosek (1998) found that faculty members are challenged to make fundamental changes to their teaching strategies as they move from classroom-based to online teaching.

What Makes an Effective Online Teacher?

Young (2006) examined student perceptions of what constituted effective online teachers. One of the most predominant themes was the ability to effectively communicate. A good online teacher communicates—consistently, regularly, and clearly. But what does effective communication look like, sound like, and feel like online? What communication skills are needed in the online environment that may not be prevalent in face-to-face environments? Online teachers also need to be *present* and *involved* in the class. Sheridan and Kelly (2010) make a distinction between being present and developing a "teacher presence." Figure 1.2 provides suggestions for developing this type of presence. (Note that many of the technology tools described in Figure 1.2 will be explored in subsequent chapters, and selected samples can be found at www.educatingliteracyteachersonline.com.)

Since the teacher is not physically present, it is especially important that his or her "presence" is felt through communication and involvement in the class. This presence is also instrumental in creating a virtual learning community. Palloff and Pratt (2007) stress that "the learning community is the vehicle through which learning occurs online. . . . Without the support and participation of a learning community, there is no online

Figure 1.2. Developing Your Teacher Presence

Developing Your Teacher Presence	Suggested Activities
Start the class with an interactive introduction	• Create a video to introduce yourself—you can use Animoto or Go!Animate • Share some photos of yourself—you can use Smilebox, Flickr, Photopeach, Photobucket • Create an auditory welcome—you can use VOKI, VoiceThread, Blabberize, yodio • Create a digital story about yourself and how you came to teaching—you can use PicLits, Pixton Comics, Go!Animate, Photostory, iMovie
Make yourself "seen" and "heard"	• Use audio/create podcasts to talk through multimedia presentations—you can use Audacity, Apple iTunes, WavePad • Have "live" meetings—you can use Wimba, Collaborate, Go to Meeting, Skype, Adobe Connect, Screencast-o-matic • Create brief video introductions to learning modules or topics—you can use a flip camera, webcam, or your phone. You can share these on password-protected sites like Vimeo or you can create a password-protected YouTube channel
Post regular announcements	• Use them to: summarize a discussion, highlight great work, post links to relevant news articles, share personal stories, or provide a "weekly overview" of the course
Add a personal touch	• Share personal stories • Use emoticons • Keep a blog where you can post additional topics and thoughts
Regularly reach out to students	• Create a spreadsheet with all students' names and a note to help you remember them (e.g., where they are from). Check off each time you interact with a student—either through a discussion or an email. Check periodically to make sure that you have interacted with each student.
Be responsive	• Reply to emails within a 24-hour period or give students a heads-up when you cannot immediately reply • Give prompt feedback on assignments
Let your students know you are there	• Check in every day, multiple times if possible. Even if they are brief, frequent checks let the student know you are there, allow you to quickly address misunderstandings, and lighten your load so the communications do not build up. • Set "live" office hours for synchronous chat or web-based face-to-face chat.
Engage in a variety of ongoing interactions	• In order for students to see you in different ways, try to vary your announcements and posts in discussions. • If you will not be "present," let students know (e.g., "I will be away for the next few days. If you don't see me as regularly as usual, don't be alarmed. I will catch up with you when I get back!")

course" (p. 29). The way we build community through communication and interaction is different when we teach online versus face to face (see more on this in Chapter 2).

In addition to the teacher behaviors that facilitate the creation of a learning community, an effective online teacher needs to think very differently about course design, with particular attention to features that encourage dynamic, engaging learning. An online teacher needs to think about ways in which design elements interact with course content to support effective teaching practices, such as engagement, modeling, questioning, and motivating students. Much of this work is done upfront before the course even begins. An effective teacher is able to create a well-organized yet flexible learning experience centered on the learner and the goals of instruction (see more on this in Chapter 4).

Finally, an effective online teacher needs to have certain technology competencies that help facilitate learning in this virtual environment. This means having a solid understanding of how technology serves the learning environment as well as how to support students through this technology. Specific competencies would include navigating networks; effectively using the Internet; creating, sending, saving, and retrieving documents in different formats; working with different Microsoft Office and Google tools; creating multimedia presentations; and using digital files, video, audio, and webpages. Building capacity in this arena is a process that requires the ability to locate and utilize resources; the willingness to explore and test, as tools change and new ones emerge; and a disposition toward collaboration (see more on this in Chapter 3). Ongoing collaboration with those who bring expertise in technology and instructional design can maximize the effectiveness of online teaching. At the same time, collaboration of this kind shifts teaching from a personal experience to one that is shared, and this shift has implications for our identities as teachers.

TENSIONS, RENEGOTIATIONS, AND CRITICAL REFLECTIONS

There are fundamental differences between face-to-face teaching and teaching in an online learning environment. One difference, according to Edwards, Perry, and Janzen (2011), is that the focus in online teaching shifts from "learning *from*" to "learning *with*" (p. 113). While learning is still rooted in a social constructivist framework, the focal point shifts from the teacher to the student, with the teacher in more of a facilitator role than ever before. Baran, Correia, and Thompson (2011) assert, "The online environment changes the fundamental nature of the interaction between the teacher, student, and content, requiring a re-examination of the roles teachers take in enhancing students' learning"

(p. 429)—the shift of power moves from the teacher onto the student without the proximity of the teacher. Moore and Kearsley (2012) point out that the teacher often does not know how a student reacts to something said or material presented unless asked for feedback or as it is reported back in an assignment. Without visual proximity and face-to-face contact, we rely more heavily on the student's initiative coupled with our preplanned methods of obtaining feedback in this type of learning environment.

The shift in the role of the teacher is compounded by the fact that many of us have not experienced models of effective online teaching. In fact, the good teachers we've experienced through our K–12 and university schooling have served as models upon which we've built our own identities of good teaching. However, many of us have not similarly had models of effective online teachers in our lives. Smith (2005) asserts that this is a barrier, as "we have not all been exposed to the techniques and methods needed to make online work successful" (p. 2). For many of us, mapping our identities on the discourses and practices of a field that is unfamiliar can cause tension and discomfort.

Moreover, unlike standing in a classroom with students in front of us, where the context for learning is physical and the players are the teacher and the student, the context for online learning is not bound by physical space and the players are not just the student and teacher but also the technology through which learning is mediated. This new dimension of technology presents new relationships and makes the teaching environment more of a system. Learning new technology tools and how to approach teaching through technology changes the dynamics of teaching. Aspden and Helm (2004) assert that as a result, online teachers need to employ new strategies that are both "high tech" and "high touch" (p. 246).

According to Major (2010), many educators feel overwhelmed by the increased demands on time that come with developing and delivering an online course or learning experience. Young (2006) asserts that, "Effective teachers have a very difficult task. In a traditional classroom, instructors can adjust content, delivery, assignments, and even the schedule as the course evolves, as they adjust to the needs of the student. An online instructor must design the course in advance; prepare material, schedules, assessments, and even discussion topics" (p. 74). This emphasis on "pre-structuring" a course can shift the dynamic of spontaneity and change our conceptions of what it means to be learner-centered.

Additionally, online teaching is labor intensive—receiving emails and posts at all times of the day, reading and responding to written discussions, providing detailed individualized written feedback, and being available outside of normal class time and office hours—requires different approaches to time management (on both the teacher's and the student's part) than those that most of us have established. Finally, Major (2010) also found that often the faculty member's role in online teaching sometimes is not as clear, the workload allocations are not always as fair, many institutions lack adequate support for online teachers, and there can be inadequate compensation for the amount of time and responsibility that come with online teaching.

While clearly there are many challenges to online teaching, there are also many advantages, and it is important to consider how the acquisition of the associated new skills and competencies impacts the renegotiation of our identities. For example, many faculty have felt rejuvenated from teaching online and have found that they appreciate the complexity and the intellectual challenge that come with engaging with new ideas, developing new skill sets, and exploring new ways of thinking about teaching and learning (Major, 2010). In addition, some online faculty have enjoyed the schedule flexibility, increased efficiency in teaching, opportunities to engage in new technologies, and exploration of getting to know students in different ways (McKenzie, Mims, Bennett, & Waugh, 2000). Furthermore, in some instances a "reverse impact" has been observed, where the result of teaching in virtual environments has improved face-to-face teaching such that teachers used more technology, employed more effective teaching strategies, and improved communication with students in their face-to-face classrooms as a result of teaching online (Roblyer, Porter, Bielefeldt, & Donaldson, 2009).

Situating the teacher at the center of online learning is certainly crucial to its success but must be done thoughtfully and with full disclosure about how teaching online changes who we are as teachers. At the beginning of the chapter we asked you to think about what makes a good teacher. Perhaps you came up with many of the criteria that were mentioned in this chapter. Hopefully, many of these criteria are ones that would describe you as a teacher. While our professional identities are rooted in how we see ourselves as teachers, they are not stagnant but are instead fluid; they are constantly shaped by the discourses and cultural practices of the environments in which we live and work. Lane has certainly changed the way in which she thinks about learning experiences before they occur and is more intentional in structuring online learning experiences to mirror what she knows about good teaching, both in the K–12 and higher education arenas. Susan was surprised to find that she gets to know her students better online because she spends more time interacting with them one on one and observing them interacting with one another than she has in previous face-to-face classes. By knowing her students better, and having a stronger sense of how they are learning, she can provide comments and questions tailored to better scaffold their understanding.

As discussions about technology, learning systems, and course enrollments tend to dominate the research on online learning, we need to make sure that we advocate for ourselves and make sure that we don't lose sight of who we are as teachers and teacher educators. We also need to apply our critical gaze to the role of online teachers. Asking ourselves questions such as "How does online teacher perception of identity impact student achievement?," "What more do we need to know about how face-to-face teachers negotiate their identities as they shift to teaching online?," "Does teacher identity impact teacher satisfaction?," and "How can we ensure that teachers are being supported as they negotiate new teaching identities?" are important in moving forward. Being aware of how our multiple identities overlap and influence one another is the first step to reflection and becoming more effective online teacher educators.

Activities to Try

- Write down three things that are important to you as a teacher—how do these look in your face-to-face teaching? How do they look in your online teaching?
- Think about the "best" teachers that you have had—what made them great?
- Think about the "best" literacy teachers that you have seen—what made them great?
- Look through the suggested activities in Figure 1.1. What new one can you try . . . or can you improve on one that you already do?

VOICES FROM THE FIELD

In my online courses, I endeavor to build a community by helping my students feel welcomed, encouraged, and valued. I begin each class by posting a welcome video and virtual classroom tour. I create this video using Camtasia screen capture software and post it on YouTube for easy access. Then I include the link in a welcome email for students who might otherwise feel lost in an online course. In addition, before the course officially begins, I post an announcement where I convey my heartfelt interest in meeting the students and my commitment to making space for their voices and lived experiences.

In addition, I use multiple different modalities to create a welcoming atmosphere within the course and to promote student engagement. Each week I use images and music clips that weave students' interests, passions, and cultures into the course. To do this, I create weekly Adobe Presentations (flash presentations created in PowerPoint with the Adobe Presenter add-in) that introduce the students to the week's readings and assignments. I begin these presentations with a music clip that both represents a student's favorite genre or artist and underscores some of the key themes in the course. One semester I had a student who adored Michael Jackson, so for one week's presentation on creating transformative classroom spaces, I integrated a music clip of the song "Man in the Mirror." In addition, in my weekly presentations, on Voice Thread, and in my group emails, I mention students by name and, with permission, integrate student quotes from the week before with images of their projects. Through these efforts, I hope to communicate how important each individual is to the online community.

Finally, I try to create opportunities to interact with students as individuals. For instance, I use a student/teacher journal for students to reflect on the readings and to consider what the readings might mean for their own practice. This journal serves as an assessment tool (both formative and summative), a way to differentiate instruction, and a space for students to speak candidly about the course topics. I also use grading as a form of appreciative inquiry where I combine constructive feedback with a sincere appreciation of students' unique talents and strengths. College students at every level seem to benefit from knowing that they are valued by their professors, their institution, and their professional communities.

—Heather Neal, assistant professor,
Sinclair Community College

CHAPTER 2

Building and Sustaining Effective Learning Communities

Questions to Ponder

- How is an online learning community different from a face-to-face learning community?
- How do online learning communities push us to do something new and different?
- How can a learning community help us share our collaborative knowledge about teaching and learning?
- How do online discussions contribute to a learning community?

If you think through your life to identify your most satisfying or rewarding learning experiences, most likely there was someone else involved in the learning process. Maybe it was one other person (a mentor, teacher, or parent), perhaps it was working with a partner to complete a project or task, or it may have been in a group. Many of our memorable learning experiences are ones that occurred in the presence of others. Being part of a learning community—whether it is one other person or a group—is a valuable part of the learning process and one that is supported by a social constructivist framework of learning.

Moving learning online does not change the importance of supporting this type of community. A learning community is the vehicle through which powerful learning occurs. Palloff and Pratt (2007) emphasize that "key to the learning process are the interactions among students themselves, the interactions between faculty and students, and the collaboration in learning that results from these interactions" (p. 4). We need to be very deliberate when creating opportunities for these interactions, especially in a space that intuitively encourages us to work on our own. We also need to see online learning communities as a new frontier for expanding how we work together. Online teacher education offers greater opportunities for cultural and geographic diversity among teacher participants, which can lead to richer understandings of sociocultural influences on literacy learning. As teachers engage in professional development and learning communities that are not geographically bound, the notion of "communities of practice" changes. By being purposeful and thoughtful about how we foster these participatory communities across wider boundaries, we can push online learning to do things that cannot be done in a context that is bound by time and space. Palloff and Pratt (2007) urge us to think about building and sustaining effective learning communities and suggest that, "without the purposeful formation of an online learning community in online learning, we are doing nothing new and different" (p. 231).

In this chapter we shift from spotlighting the role of the teacher (Chapter 1) to exploring how to create rich, diverse online learning communities. While building communities of practice is important in any online environment, they are particularly important in literacy education that is deeply rooted in a social constructivist philosophy. While this chapter addresses building learning communities in a broad sense, literacy-specific examples highlight how a learning community can be foregrounded as an essential dimension of an online teaching and learning experience in this discipline. Through the remainder of this chapter we will address why a learning community is important, explore strategies for creating communities, and discuss how online discussion can create a context for supporting a community of learners. We believe that a successful learning experience in literacy will be supported through learning communities, as they have the potential to increase students' learning and engagement as well as model what we know about best practice in literacy education.

THE IMPORTANCE OF LEARNING COMMUNITIES

Establishing a learning community is as important in an online class as it is in a face-to-face class. In online education the development of a learning community has been linked to student satisfaction, retention, and learning. Learning communities help tie students to learning and pull students into the course content. Others have demonstrated the importance of learning communities through research in distance education and also teacher development. Palloff and Pratt (2007) assert that "the power of a learning community . . . supports the intellectual as well as personal growth and development of its members" (p. 232). Learning communities in teacher education have also proven to be powerful experiences, as Dunne, Nave, and Lewis (2000) found that participation in learning communities not only resulted in changes to teaching practices but also increased teachers' involvement, ownership, innovation, and leadership. Furthermore, Sherer, Shea, and Kristensen (2003) found that through participating in professional online communities, teachers met new colleagues and enhanced their knowledge of teaching. In a face-to-face environment, sustaining these communities is a bit easier since you are usually guaranteed to see one another in person on a regular basis. However, in an online classroom we need to support these communities a bit differently in order to use them to their maximum potential. The inclusion of learning communities in educating literacy teachers online is an essential piece of effective instruction, and therefore we will elaborate on this connection through the remainder of the chapter.

Brown (2001) identified three stages of community building in online courses, noting that as groups went through each of these stages, their level of engagement increased. Brown's first stage is getting acquainted. It is important that members in a learning community get to know one another and explore the commonalities that link them as a group. A learning community needs this foundation to move forward as they grow and learn together. The second stage occurs as a learning community becomes more connected through longer discussions and increased interaction. This is where group members become more interdependent and support one another's learning. Finally, the last stage is a sense of camaraderie where friendship and relationships develop. It is important that when groups reach this stage they have some sort of vehicle for maintaining this relationship after the learning experience is over (it could be a Facebook page, a blog, or a Listserv). In order for groups to go through these stages it is necessary for groups to have an established purpose and clarity of expectations. Brown (2001) also found that the instructor plays a key role in the development of an online community through modeling, encouragement, and participation (our role in fostering a learning community is more than just setting one up!).

SETTING UP A LEARNING COMMUNITY

There are several considerations in establishing learning communities in our online environments. First, we need to think through how our learning communities will communicate—maybe through discussion boards, or blogs, or real-time meetings. We need to think through how our course design and activities support this communication (this will be further explored later in the chapter). Also, we need to consider how the phases of the learning community can support student-to-student interaction that reinforces course content. Finally, we need to be clear to communicate our expectations for how we will engage and interact in these learning communities. It is important to reiterate that teachers need to be a key part of these learning communities. Palloff and Pratt (2007) assert that learning communities are more effective when the instructor is part of the learning community—this means that we not only need to set up these communities, but also carefully think through how we communicate and interact within these social engagements.

Remember that the teacher needs to be a valuable member of this community. You have the responsibility of modeling how to engage in a learning community. There are many ways you can do this throughout a course. For example, posting announcements is a good way to bring the group together. There are many times you can post announcements— these can be weekly to-do lists, biweekly summations, or unscheduled announcements whenever you see things that need to be addressed. You can also create videos or audio so that your students can hear and see you as well as "see" you in a written form. Another way of developing community is to have a space for conversations that are not part of the regular class—for example, maybe include a discussion thread specifically called "Water Cooler Chat." Discussions in the Water Cooler Chat space can be about the weather, babies, personal life, or just teaching ideas that are not directly related to the course material.

It is important to remember that even though you are encouraging student ownership in learning, the teacher still is a principle player in both the setup and the cultivation of an online community. Instructors should take active steps to foster a positive learning community. We will discuss three such steps in detail: using introductions or "Getting Started" activities, managing small-group work, and promoting reflection.

Building Community Through "Getting Started" Activities

Recently Lane was invited to be part of a study group about issues of content area literacy. There were about 12 teachers and reading specialists from various districts around the state seated at the table. Once everyone sat down, the facilitator launched right into the meeting without introductions. It was clear that the people in this group did not know one another. To Lane this felt very strange not to know anything about who the people were sitting around the table. Because of this she was not as engaged in the meeting as she might otherwise have been. This experience emphasized how important it is to spend time at the beginning of group formation to get to know those around you. This is true of an online learning experience as well. The first stage of engaging in a learning community is to spend some time at the beginning getting to know one another. There are many online ways to facilitate introductions. While posting introductory personal statements is most common, this is not the only way, and sometimes reading 20 introduction messages can get a bit tedious! Introductions that relate directly to the content are most effective. For example, it is especially powerful when you can tie these activities to a literacy goal. In Figure 2.1 we suggest some literacy-specific introduction activities. Icebreakers can pull students into the content and facilitate the forming of learning communities.

Figure 2.1. Literacy Icebreakers

Getting Started Activity	Description
Building a class Shelfari	You can create a class Shelfari account (supported by Amazon.com) and have each student post his or her favorite book and discuss it.
Making Animoto videos	Students can make short free (30-second) videos introducing themselves.
Making Voki videos	Students can create a Voki (an animated character) to represent themselves and then record an audio introduction.
Using Smilebox to create montages	Students can create a photo collage of themselves or their classrooms and share this using Smilebox.
Making Wordles	Students can create and describe a word cloud of words that are important to them.
Reading interest survey	Students can take an online reading interest inventory and share what they learned about themselves.
If you were on a deserted island and you could only bring one book, what book would you bring?	You can create a Wiki or Google Doc to keep a list of these books—not only will you learn about your students through their book choices but, you will also create a great recommended book list!
Share a social bookmarking page—this will let others know which websites you go to and enable them to learn about who you are	You can share one another's social bookmarking sites to learn about one another and learn about some new websites as well!
"A Day in the Life"—display how literacy looks in your life (you can use either real pictures or Google images)	This is a great way to capture the many different types of literacy activities that we engage in on a daily basis.

Building Community Through Small-Group Assignments

While it is wonderful to interact online with a diverse group of people, it can be overwhelming when a group gets too large. Whole-class discussions can work in face-to-face environments but can get pretty unwieldy online. As a result, it is a good idea to balance large-group assignments with small-group assignments. Silvers, O'Connell, and Fewell (2007) found that "When our students were placed in small work groups (e.g. similar content groups, or groups based on selected inquiry questions) they became more connected and felt less like strangers in the class" (p. 82).

Group work in a face-to-face setting is something we are familiar with—it is easy to see when one person is going to talk by looking at body language or facial expressions. Usually the group leader emerges quickly and we can tell when someone needs to be invited to speak or seems disengaged. This is not as obvious in online groups. This is a new space for group work and we cannot assume that our familiar patterns for getting things done will be generalized to this different setting. Managing small-group work online can be difficult. It is important that we help groups negotiate group processes before they start working—especially since the norms and routines are not as established or familiar in an online setting.

One thing we can do to start off groups is to address norms, roles, and routines. We can do this using a fishbowl technique, in which one group participates in a discussion while the rest of the group watches from the outside to observe the process. After the discussion is over, the rest of the group debriefs on what they observed, including what seemed to go well and how the discussion could have been improved. We can also provide checkpoints for the group processes. Some things we can do to help support groups include the following:

- Assign a team leader.
- Engage in process checks.
- Set group goals when appropriate.
- Encourage a group thank you at the end.
- Provide space for an individual and group self-evaluation.

It is also important that we help groups set expectations for group work. The following are some questions that groups can address before starting their work (adapted from Palloff and Pratt, 2007, pp. 165–166):

- How will the group communicate?
- What roles will group members have?
- What day will discussion begin?
- How quickly should group members respond?
- How will the group handle a member who is not participating?

Many of us are used to group work but not online group work where you cannot "see" your classmates. Being clear about these expectations will lead to more productive and more satisfying group work. It is also important that we think through how our smaller groups will interact with the larger group so that we avoid a fractured learning community.

Building Community Through Reflection

As we think about online learning communities we have to recognize that this context may be new and unfamiliar to many of those involved. While the goals of a learning community are similar to a face-to-face class, because the setting is different it is important that we engage our students in reflective activities as they develop their online learning community skills and practices. Brown (2001) suggests that we do this multiple times in a semester where we ask learners to reflect on questions such as "What have you contributed to the community?," "What have others done to help you feel more a part of a community?," "What has this learning community accomplished?," "What does it still need to attain?" (p. 33). As we become more adept at being online, we are interacting in many more online communities (i.e., Facebook, blogs, Pinterest, etc. . . .). However, there is a difference between a social community and a learning community and sometimes this line can be blurred by the technology that mediates both of these communities. It is important that we engage our students in a "double loop" (Palloff & Pratt, 2007) of learning, where they reflect on the learning process as much as the learning itself. By having students think about how they learn in an online community, they will not only increase the amount that they learn but also improve how they engage with others in this setting.

ONLINE DISCUSSIONS SUPPORTING LEARNING COMMUNITIES

Picture that you are sitting at a table with a group of colleagues—you are discussing something that has happened at work today. How does this discussion go? Who talks first? Who talks the most/the least? How do you negotiate turn-taking in the discussion? What role do you tend to play in discussions? Do you ask questions? Give your own examples? Offer opinions?

In some ways, online discussions are similar to the face-to-face discussions that we have every day. In online discussions we still negotiate roles. We still make decisions about what we are going to contribute to the discussion and how we will participate. We still have our own personal comfort zones in how we discuss—however, online discussions are also very different. For one, most online discussions take place asynchronously—meaning not at the same time. For example, you can start a discussion and then the next person may not respond for perhaps a whole day. You can also read a discussion and take some time to think about what you are going to say before you participate (maybe you can think of many occasions when this would have been a good idea in some face-to-face discussions that you have been in). Also, most online discussions are done through text. That gives you time to think a bit more as you type or change what you are planning on saying as you respond. It also lets you read and reread what others have said in the discussion before you. Online discussions tend to be more formal and more academic in nature. Many of us are comfortable at a table talking with our colleagues at work, but once the same conversation occurs online it can take on a totally different tone.

While the above discussion around a table at work may seem familiar, many of us are new to online discussions. We need to think differently about how we create these discursive spaces in our online classrooms as well as how we help our students negotiate these spaces. As mentioned, there are some similarities that will help us move into these new discursive formats, but we also have to be fully aware of the differences in order to use these discussions in the most powerful way possible.

Studying and thinking about online discussions is a new frontier for teaching and learning online, and an especially interesting one for literacy education. As we explore how language mediates learning in this new discursive environment we will learn much more about online discussions. As literacy educators—whose medium is language and discourse—this is especially fertile ground for research and implications for practice. We hope that this section on online discussions will give you some guidelines to start or increase the effectiveness of this practice, but at the same time we hope that this will also inspire new areas of research and thinking.

Guidelines About Online Discussions

Online discussions may be one of the most important parts of the online learning experience. They are a way to ensure that students are engaged and present. Shea, Frederickson, Pickett, and Peltz (2004) found that students reported putting more thought into online discussion postings than they did in a face-to-face classroom discussion and that they were more likely to participate in an online discussion (p. 9). Haggerty et al. (2001) also found that online discussions promoted greater cognitive and exploratory learning, while Rovai (2004) found that discussions support more student-to-student conversation and collaboration. Because of the importance of online discussions to this learning environment we need to spend a lot of time thinking through this setting. Online discussions also contribute to a learning community because they allow for an exchange of ideas, promote engagement with others, facilitate consensus building, and support collaborative critical thinking. While there are many reasons to use online discussions, they will not be effective if we do not give our students clear expectations about how they are to engage in these discussions.

Wang and Chen (2008) assert that while online discussions have the potential for supporting higher-level thinking and engagement, it is hard to sustain cognitive presence over time; thus the development of rules and expectations are essential. They developed guidelines that they found stimulated active involvement and led to increased cognitive presence. Their rules to students included giving them start and cutoff dates, establishing a minimal number of posts, requiring that they supported their arguments with evidence, encouraging them to keep one point per short message (and if no one answers their posting, send invitations to three classmates for responses), not allowing them to post before a second deadline, encouraging them to build on existing ideas by quoting and paraphrasing other people's messages, and finally, if they have nothing more to add, giving them guidelines for wrapping up nicely with a concise summary (pp. 162–163).

When you think through setting up an online discussion you need to establish some guidelines up front about engaging in discussions. Consider the following questions when establishing your expectations:

- What is your expectation for timing of posts?
- How long should an initial post be?
- How long should responses be?
- How many posts meet minimum criteria? Exemplary performance?
- How many posts should each participant contribute?
- How many comments to group members' posts should each participant contribute?
- Is there a length that is desired for response posts?
- How should the post be structured—reference to text, reference to experience, reference to other posts, follow-up questions?

When Lane started teaching online she began with a checklist for online discussions. This evolved over many semesters. She began to think about what participation looked like in a real-time discussion. It occurred to her that she does not always respond to every person in a discussion with a lengthy response and it was unreasonable to expect this of her students. Also, people often just want to know that they have been listened to. Rovai (2007) found that many students sometimes felt that writing in forums was like writing a message, placing it in a bottle, and throwing it out to sea.

There are also many different rubrics that you can use for your online discussions (see Appendix B: Discussion Rubrics). It is important that you either find one or develop one that fits your expectations for discussions. Establishing clear expectations is the first important step in managing effective online discussions.

Creating Robust Discussion Prompts

While it is important to give our students guidelines for participation, it is also just as crucial to give them discussions that they *want* to participate in. In analyzing different types of online discussions, Wang and Chen (2008) asserted that these spaces had the potential for higher-level and critical thinking but could also support ineffective practices. They further asserted that "without proper design and structure, students took on a passive role in the discussions . . . and their cognitive engagement was low" (p. 157). Wang and Chen believe that if designed successfully, online discussions could support cognitive, social, and teacher presence (p.159). In order to support higher-level thinking, one of the keys is to start with the right question or prompt. It is important that discussions start with an open-ended question. These questions are best geared toward the higher levels of Bloom's taxonomy, a progression of thinking skills that begin at the lower level and move to a higher level, such as application, analysis, synthesis, and evaluation.

Coming up with the right question can be tricky but can lead to powerful conversations. We can think of many prompts that we have used that have either flopped or led to less than desirable lower-level discussions. It takes trial and error as well as careful thinking to come up with an effective prompt.

Prompts that stimulate discussion. Creating a good question takes time. First, it is important to ask open-ended questions—ones that do not have a single right or wrong answer. It is also effective to play devil's advocate, where you probe students to think against their usual way of thinking or out of their comfort zone. Another way of thinking about questions is to ask students questions that belong to one of these three categories: *convergent, divergent,* and *evaluative* thinking. When we ask students *convergent* questions we are probing them to think through the why and how. For example, giving students an example of a struggling reader and some background information and testing data might inspire a why question: "Why do you think this student is struggling?" or "How can the teacher take this information and plan effective instruction?" When we ask students *divergent* questions we want students to predict, imagine, or think broadly. For example, we might give students a piece of text and have them come up with different ways to teach this text or have them re-create their writing block if they did not have any constraints on time and money. Finally, we can ask students *evaluative* questions where we encourage them to defend, justify, or judge. Perhaps we ask students to make a placement recommendation for a student given information about his or her academic and social development, or have them consider the strengths and weaknesses of a certain state reading legislation.

Prompts that foster different perspectives. Another way to inspire good discussions is to have students take different perspectives on an issue or assume different roles. One way to do this is to use de Bono's (1985) "Six Hat" metaphor for thinking, where each participant wears a different metaphorical hat to discuss an issue. The six hats that he suggested are as follows (but you can create your own hats and hat colors as it fits your purpose):

- *White Hat:* Objective figures and facts—neutrality. This person deals with the factual information and asks questions based on the given facts, needed facts, and what the data say.
- *Red Hat:* Emotions and feelings. This person taps into the emotional piece of this issue.
- *Black Hat:* Difficulties, dangers, and potential problems. This person considers the risks and the potential problems of an issue.
- *Yellow Hat:* Hope, optimism, positive thinking. This person is the optimist and points out the benefits or the bright side.
- *Green Hat:* Creativity and new ideas. This person tries to think about new perspectives or alternate solutions.
- *Blue Hat:* Managing the thinking. This person is in charge of facilitating the group process and keeping the group on track.

One way you could use this "Six Hat" metaphor would be to find an issue and have each student look at this from a different perspective. For example, you could have students explore the "3rd Grade Guarantee" that all students will be able to read by 3rd grade or they will not be promoted. This topic could be explored through each of these hats and then each group would submit a summary of these perspectives at the end of the discussion.

Prompts that inspire debate. We can also create prompts based on controversial issues and ask students to discuss from a certain perspective. This has to be carefully managed, however, as students may need to be reminded of online netiquette and the importance of thinking before responding. It is also best to pick issues that have multiple sides. For example, teachers can debate Seattle's MAPS testing boycott, or what the Common Core State Standards mean for instruction. What are the costs? (See Appendix A: Assignment 1 for debate assignment.)

Prompts based on case studies. Another assignment that has promoted higher-level thinking and discursive engagement is the use of case studies. Case studies encourage collaborative literacy problem solving, emphasize active and cooperative learning, and support higher-order thinking. Lane added case studies to her online discussions in order to raise the level of conversation for her students (see Figure 2.2).

Hsu (2004) found that using case studies in teacher education helped students become aware of their assumptions, consider multiple perspectives, develop plans of action, apply principles of learning, and gain confidence as professionals. Having students discuss around a case study could be a wonderful way to manage an online discussion (see Appendix A: Assignment 2 for an example of a case study).

Supporting Good Discussion

Creating clear expectations and providing a meaningful reason for discussing are two essential pieces of supporting meaningful online discussions. There are other things you can do to ensure that these discursive spaces are effective. Being aware of your participation, helping students become aware of their participation, and giving students more responsibilities in these conversations are all ways to support powerful online discussions.

Teacher participation. As previously mentioned, for many of us online discussions are not natural and therefore sometimes we need to take the time to help our students develop the competencies that will help them be more effective in these settings. We need to be aware of how we participate in these discussions in an effort to support our students. First, it is important to make your presence known, but not to dominate these discussions. Just like in face-to-face discussions, an overly talkative instructor can squelch discussion. Our role is to set the conditions for the students to do the talking. Another thing an instructor can do is summarize key points from a discussion or draw connections between the discussions and the content. Weaving in student comments encourages students and communicates to them that you have read their discussion. Additionally, we can model the format for discussions. It is best to discuss in multiple short paragraphs and bulleted lists, as long rambling paragraphs are harder to read. Outing and Ruel (2004) found that students spent considerably more time reading and remembering the content of shorter paragraphs online than they did longer ones.

Student responsibility. We can also encourage students to take more responsibility in these discussions. For example, you can give students roles in discussions, such as summarizing a discussion, generating a topic, or creating an assertion and soliciting comments. You can also have

Figure 2.2. Spotlight on the Evolution of Online Discussions: Lane's Move to Using Case Studies

Reason for Evolution	Desire for Higher-Level Discussions
Motivation to Change	When I first started teaching online I found myself falling into the trap of assigning chapters to read and then asking a general question, such as, "What are some takeaways that you have from the chapter that relate to your understanding of this concept?" "How did this chapter relate to your own teaching?" "While this seemed like an easy way to manage multiple chapters and multiple discussions and put the learning on the laps of the students to discuss, it also did not generate the critical thinking that I was hoping to accomplish in my online classes. Basically the discussions were boring and turned into a show-and-tell of what everyone was doing in their own classrooms (which is not a bad thing but was inspiring more of the practitioner and less of the scholarly behaviors that I was trying to promote).
Revision	When I revised one of my courses, I decided to give my discussions an overhaul and used the online discussions as a place to really go beyond the sharing time that my previous general questions were encouraging. In order to participate in a discussion around the case studies, students had to integrate knowledge gained from multiple materials (video, reading, web resources) and then take on a certain perspective. They also were asked to analyze one another's posts and synthesize one another's ideas. In addition, instead of taking turns and sharing, they needed to build on one another's ideas. This was a much richer way to use online discussions.
Process	While in theory this shift seemed like a no-brainer, in practice it was very time consuming. First, I wanted students to discuss in grade-level groups. Our program is K–12. While there are points at which cross-grade discussions are important, there are other times when, in order to be the most meaningful, students need to discuss issues in groups of similar grade levels. The easiest way for me to break up the groups was to create elementary, middle, and secondary groupings. However, that meant I needed to create case studies for each level. While I tried to keep the content similar and the learning objectives similar I needed to find videos, readings, and web resources at each grade level. This was time consuming.
	Next, I wanted to make sure that I communicated expectations clearly. Therefore, I developed a template for the case studies that would be used in all three groups and for all of the case studies. Consistency is important in online teaching, and therefore it was important for these templates to be the same each time (see Appendix A: Assignment 2 for example).
Outcome	By creating more engaging content and establishing clear expectations, I transformed my online discussions into a more powerful place for thinking, learning, and collaboration. The time was well spent!!

students take turns facilitating a discussion around a topic. Perhaps at the beginning of a course you can have a sign-up sheet of topics. Students can sign up for each topic, present on this topic, and facilitate a conversation around this topic. Giving students these responsibilities helps them take ownership and become more active members in their learning community. Some roles that your students can take include the following:

- *Facilitator:* Initiates discussion, oversees knowledge, organizes flow of discussion
- *Critical friend:* Analyzes and critiques posts, promotes deeper thinking, engages the rest of the group
- *Content manager:* Makes sure that the content is being reflected and adds new content to the discussion
- *Summarizer:* Summarizes and reflects on the discussion

Student reflection in discussion. Students also need to be aware of their participation in discussion. There are a few ways you can have them do this. You can have them explicitly reflect on their participation. For example, in one class Lane had her students analyze and reflect on their participation in group discussions (Clarke, 2012). After one period of online discussions she asked the students to go back into this discussion and engage in an *individual analysis, group analysis,* and *goal setting.* For the individual analysis the students were asked to think about the quantity of their posts. Specifically, they were asked to tabulate how many posts they contributed to the discussion, as well as the length of these posts. Students were also asked to look at the quality of their initial posts and contributions to other students' posts. They also engaged in a group analysis and then they established two discussion goals for themselves. At the end of the next discussion the students went back to the discussion and reflected upon the goals that they set for themselves. By engaging in a self-reflection of asynchronous discussions the students became more aware of how these discussions could contribute to increased engagement, reflection, and deep learning.

Another way you could have students reflect on their practice is to have them code their own discussions. Williams, Rose, and Heineke (2012) had their students code their own discussions to facilitate their understanding of what constitutes meaning making during discussion. They used codes around the topics of relationship building (affirming, thanking, joking), restating (rewording or summarizing), expounding (explaining, justifying, giving an opinion), questioning, and challenging. Supporting students' own critical self-reflection is a wonderful way to empower them to learn more about online discussions and their own participation.

Finally, you can also have students rate their own posts—similar to an Amazon rating system. You can have students indicate which posts were most helpful, most stimulating, most provocative, or most inspiring. By helping students be more reflective, we can increase the effectiveness of online discussions as a powerful learning tool!

TENSIONS, RENEGOTIATIONS, AND CRITICAL REFLECTIONS

As we explore the new terrain of online learning communities there are tensions that we must navigate. We need to think critically about how we can take the best parts of a learning community and move them online. Asking ourselves what are the differences and what challenges we face are good first steps. We also need to consider how we situate ourselves in online learning communities. When we teach face-to-face and we break our students into small work groups, we usually are not members of each of these working groups. However, often when groups meet online, teachers can feel that they need to be present in group interactions. This can be a *lot* of text for online instructors to manage and can quickly become overwhelming. Finding the place for the instructor that balances guidance and coaching without being overly involved is a tension that many online educators can experience. One thing that can be done is to provide summary feedback on a whole discussion rather than commenting on each thread. Summary feedback considers the group's conversation as a whole and allows the instructor to note themes, expand on important ideas, and raise constructive questions within the context of the discussion. This summary feedback does not have to be written; rather, it can be in video or audio form.

Building and sustaining online learning communities also requires a certain amount of renegotiation. Creating virtual learning communities is an important—and necessary—component to online learning. Much of the powerful thinking that our students do takes place within this social context. Barab, Schatz, and Scheckler (2004) assert that building online communities in the service of learning is a major accomplishment about which we have much to learn. Finding ways to harness this space for powerful learning can take some new thinking about student roles and responsibilities. It also must take some consideration of how we not only set up these learning communities, but how we facilitate these spaces.

Finally, we must be critical about how these communities grow and develop. We have learned a lot about how to build and support learning communities online. We can go through the stages of learning communities, reflect on our own practices, support students' reflection, organize small groups, and create powerful discursive spaces. However, we are still in the infancy of understanding how online communities function and are sustained. Barab, Schatz, and Scheckler (2004) emphasize that "we are currently in an exciting time in which pedagogical theory and technological advances have created an opportunity to design innovative and powerful environments to support learning" (p. 200). However, with this exciting time comes the necessity of considering how we negotiate these "diverse" participatory contexts in ways that build on the strengths of this diversity. We need to figure out how we set up experiences that capture rich cross-regional/cultural interactions. We need to push ourselves to continue to think about how pedagogy and technology intersect and how we can continue to create even more effective collaborative learning environments. We hope that together we will push forward our thinking about building and sustaining effective learning communities.

Activities to Try

- Think of a new introductory activity that ties into your content.
- Develop a new small-group activity and think through how you will set this up and how the small groups will function in relation to the whole learning community.
- Include a group self-reflection to build community.
- Look at the rubrics in Appendix B; revise one that you have used or create a new one.
- Develop a new discussion prompt.
- Develop a case study.
- Have your students analyze or code one of their discussions.
- Try a fishbowl setup, where you have a group discuss and other groups observe and reflect on this discussion.
- Analyze your own participation in online discussions.

VOICES FROM THE FIELD

I came to online teaching as a professor who had been doing work with course management systems to one degree or another for the past 21 years. Many elements of my courses were online to some degree (chat rooms, blogs, discussion boards, postings of syllabi, articles, podcasts, videos, and drop boxes for submission of student work to be graded and returned). Recently I moved most of this to more highly interactive learning modules that students used to teach themselves, evaluate themselves, and then engage in group projects, wikis, blogs, and/or live discussion boards. The shift to a more hybrid model allowed me to incorporate many of the e-skills I wanted my students to use along with the ability to still meet with them in both a virtual learning environment and a traditional bricks-and-mortar classroom. Most recently, I have found that many more of my undergraduate and graduate students have turned to their iPads, tablets, notebooks, and Kindles to access textbooks, rather than purchase expensive print editions. These new e-textbooks still allow students ways to interact with the text (e.g., highlighting, note-taking, bookmarking items that are of interest and/or concern to them).

I found that many of the tools provided with Blackboard Learn, the course management system being used at my university, were appropriate for my teaching and my students' learning. These tools allowed me to easily incorporate YouTube videos, online testing modules, podcasts, and case studies. The modules I created with these tools allowed students to learn at their own pace, self-evaluate their learning, participate with the classroom colleagues in online discussions, and work cooperatively between online and on-campus course meetings to better help them understand the materials. Having the ability to provide "virtual" office hours for my students also provided another outlet in their busy schedules to meet with me without having to come to campus.

My thinking about the value of using technology in higher education has not really changed. I see the use of technology as another tool to augment my teaching and my students' learning; I do not view the technology as a full replacement for my responsibilities toward my students' education. In my opinion, good pedagogy is good pedagogy, but using tools that will engage student learning online needs to be supportive of what I want to accomplish. I am always looking for new technologies to incorporate into my teaching, and it is not unusual for one or more of my students to approach me with a technology tool or app that they have discovered to have me try out with the class.

—Kenneth J. Weiss, professor emeritus of reading and language arts,
Central Connecticut State University

CHAPTER 3

Technology Tools That Promote Active, Constructive, and Social Learning

Questions to Ponder

- What technology tools are you using to facilitate learning?
- How has your technology use changed over the past few years—both personally and professionally?
- How do the tools that you use position your students in relation to learning?
- What factors do you consider when choosing technology tools?

Imagine that you are given a camera and asked to capture images of all of the literacy activities in which you engage in a single day. Perhaps you wake up in the morning and read the paper or listen to the news. Or perhaps you get your news on an iPad or computer. On your way to work you might listen to a podcast or the radio. You may have your phone synched to your Facebook account or email (or multiple email accounts) so you can slyly check this during the day. At work you may be engaged in various texts—fiction, nonfiction, digital texts—or you may be writing in different genres (most likely much of this will be on a computer). If you think through a day in your life, surely you will see the intersection between literacy and the many technology tools that mediate our engagement with literacy. Exactly how we engage in literacy has changed immensely with the proliferation of technology into our everyday worlds. Computers, iPads, blogs, social media, and websites are just a few of the new technologies that simultaneously offer new literacy opportunities and require new literacy skills, strategies, dispositions, and social practices. We have shifted our mind-set regarding how we define literate practices, and we are constantly adding to our technology tool repertoire. Coiro, Knobel, Lankshear, and Leu (2009) posit that "literacy will also include knowing how and when to make wise decisions about which technologies and which forms and functions of literacy most support one's purposes" (p. 5).

As we further expand our definition of literacy we also need to think about how the technology tools that we use in online learning environments support and compliment this new vision of literacy. Miller (2011) asserts that "As instructors today, we have literally at our fingertips a vast and growing body of course-relevant content which can expand student learning opportunities unimaginably beyond those provided in the conventional text and lecture-based classroom" (p. 1). It is exciting and empowering to have so many tools at our disposal to enhance learning, but it can also be overwhelming. While technology integration makes sense in today's digital world, we must carefully consider how we implement it. We need to explore technology as tools that promote active, constructive, and social learning in our online environments. Research shows that media-based learning materials can help students better relate to course concepts (Berk, 2009); however, we also want to use these tools not just to enhance content learning but also to help our students develop new literacy skills and competencies.

In the previous chapters we highlighted the importance of foregrounding the teacher and social interaction in online learning. We want to make clear that technology should be used to support this belief in learning rather than "drive" our teaching. This chapter is based on using technology as a tool—one chosen by the teacher and used for the purpose of learning, given a social constructivist framework.

TECHNOLOGY AS A TOOL

We believe that technology is a tool that mediates learning. This notion is rooted in sociocultural learning theory, first posited by Vygotsky (1962). Vygotsky believed that learning is always mediated by cultural and psychological tools. It is through these tools that we can interact in more powerful and functional ways and thus enhance learning. The first tool that we use in the development of cognitive processes is language. However, as we engage with our environment with more sophistication we constantly are appropriating other tools to facilitate more complex learning experiences. Technology can be seen as one of these tools that we use to mediate learning. However, technology itself as a contribution to learning is rapidly growing in its potential.

For those of us who are digital "immigrants" (Prensky, 2001), we can still remember learning to type on a typewriter, taking film to a store to be developed, having to make a phone call on a phone attached to a wall, and getting our news from the newspaper! These images are things of the past and certainly not part of the collective memories of the digital "natives"

(Prensky, 2001) who have grown up with computers, iPads, smartphones, and Google. There are no longer steep barriers to technology integration—anyone with a phone can make a video, any computer hooked to the Internet can create online content, and many tools are free. While technology tools have become simplified—and there are how-to videos and tutorials on almost every tool out there—just having the tools at our fingertips does not mean that we are appropriating them in a way to enhance learning. Amiel and Reeves (2008) insisted that technology should support complex human, social, and cultural interactions rather than act as a dumb servant. We need to think about these tools as facilitators of learning and as vehicles through which learning occurs. We need to be explicit about how technology fosters the development of new literacies and how this contributes both to our learning and that of our students.

While incorporating technology into online teaching and learning seems like a natural fit, the process is not as simple as one would expect due to the medium through which we are teaching. Amory (2012) suggests that many Learning Management Systems (LMS) actually do not support innovative interactive collaborative experiences because the design of these systems foregrounds content, technical issues, and information versus learning process (p. 2). It is easy to replicate a traditional one-directional didactic learning paradigm in an online setting, and we have to be careful not to be tricked into thinking that technology on its own leads to an engaging learning experience. When we think of online learning we need to be thinking about learning *through/with* technology—not just learning *from* technology. Viewing technology as a tool that mediates learning will help us enhance our students' learning in powerful ways.

TOOLS THAT SUPPORT ACTIVE LEARNING

Good teaching, good learning, and good technology all rely on the same thing—students who are active and in control of their own learning. We need to make sure that the technology we use in our classrooms supports this active engagement by the students. While we may use some wonderful technology tools in our classrooms, we need to be thoughtful about how these tools can be used to position our students as learners. Johnson (2012) reflected on her experience as an online learner in a paper given at the Literacy Research Association conference. She highlighted four online courses in which she was a student and did a comparative analysis of her own experiences. One of her criteria of analysis was how she was positioned in the course through the instructor's use of technology. She noticed that in some courses the technology tools positioned her as a *producer* of new knowledge, whereas in other courses, the technology tools used positioned her as a *consumer* of information. She reported getting the most satisfaction when she was positioned as a producer of knowledge and could use technology to empower and control her learning. When we use technology as a learning tool we need to think about how these tools position the learner in relation to learning. For example, when we ask our students to watch videos, read a text online, go to a website, or look at images, we are just asking them to be consumers of technology. While they may be more engaged as a result of having some more control over when they start and stop the video or what images they view, we are not asking them to participate in the new literacy practices that push them to actively create or synthesize new knowledge, incorporate new practices, or develop new dispositions. However, when we use technology to position our students as producers of knowledge we are supporting more constructive and active learning stances by our students. For example, having them create an original artifact by making a digital story or creating their own iMovie, taking multiple images and creating a new image, synthesizing their knowledge into a digital portfolio, or creating a training module for other students are all ways of using technology to support the active production of new knowledge. Technology is uniquely situated to support this innovative and engaging stance of knowledge production in that it is not static or one dimensional. We have to be careful not to be blinded by the bells and whistles of technology integration in the name of using technology, but rather to think through how the tools that we choose support new literacy skills. When we purposefully use technology to support active learning, we increase the learning experiences of our students.

TOOLS THAT SUPPORT CONSTRUCTIVE LEARNING

If our goal is to use technology to facilitate active learning and position our students as producers of knowledge, we need to think through the tools that we use and how they support the learning we desire. Matching tools to learning is key to successful technology integration in online teaching. Just like any other tool, different technology applications support different thinking and learning tasks. One approach to integrating technology has been to adapt the levels of thinking suggested by Benjamin Bloom (1956) into a *Bloom's Digital Taxonomy* (Churches, 2009) hierarchy where technology tools are correlated to different levels of thinking.

This hierarchy is not meant to prescribe which technology tool should be used at each stage—especially since tools are rapidly changing and growing—but rather to help teachers think through what level of thinking is desired and then to match the tool with this level. Like Bloom's hierarchy, the stages start at a lower level and move upwards to capture higher-order thinking skills. When we match tools to these levels of thinking it is important to note that many of these tools can be used to support a variety of levels. Below, some of these tools will be explained as they best meet the skills or thinking processes that categorize each level of thinking. The tool list that corresponds to each level is just a list of recommendations for illustrative purposes only—there are many other tools that can be used at each level and for different purposes. Technology is ever changing, and while the figures included in this chapter highlight some wonderful tools, there are constantly more being created. We will update those which fit each category in the online companion to this text (www.educatingliteracyteachersonline.com).

Remembering

The first level of Bloom's taxonomy is the lowest level of thinking. This is where you are asking students to remember facts and information. This surface-level recall of facts sometimes stands on its own or sometimes provides a foundation upon which higher-level skills can be applied. This knowledge-level memory of facts can be enhanced through a variety of technology tools (see Figure 3.1).

Understanding

The next level of thinking requires students to go a bit farther than just remembering facts. Now we want students to explain, categorize and annotate, showing that they have understood what they have learned. While this is also a lower level of thinking, it takes learning to the next level of complexity (see Figure 3.2).

Applying

The layers of knowledge are built upon one another and as you move up this hierarchy, students' thinking becomes more complex. In this level you are asking students to take what they are learning and apply it in different situations. You want them to present, demonstrate, simulate, or connect knowledge. For our students, this can mean taking different teaching strategies and thinking through how they would look in their own instructional settings. There are many technology tools that support this level (see Figure 3.3).

Figure 3.1. Tools for Remembering

Tool	Examples	Description	Literacy Application
Word Clouds	Wordle Tagxedo	These sites generate textual clouds using different words.	Have students create a wordle given a specific concept or vocabulary word.
Social Bookmarking	Diigio Del.icio.us	Social bookmarking is a tool that enables you to organize the websites that you visit.	Have students pick a topic and then create a social bookmarking page displaying websites on this topic.
Podcasts	iTunes International Reading Association (IRA) Literacy 2.0 (BAM Radio Network)	Podcasts are audio texts that can be listened to through the computer or on a portable MP3 or iPad/iPod.	Have students listen to some of the podcasts found on the IRA website.
Quiz Making	Classmarker Flashcard machine Quizlet	These tools allow you to make quizzes and flashcards to help memorize facts.	Give students a list of concepts to study using one of these tools.
Photo Gathering	Flickr Smilebox Photobucket	These sites are for online storage and sharing of photographs.	Have students upload or view images. This would be good for having students take photos of literacy events that they see in their everyday lives.
Videos	YouTube Teaching Channel Teacher Tube	These are video-sharing sites where teachers can share video resources.	Have students watch a video on conducting a writing workshop conference.
Web Searching	Google Bing Yahoo	These search engines are the most popular. There are also some search engines geared for kids. These allow us to find information through gathering relevant websites on a topic.	Have students pick a topic—such as fluency development—and have them do an Internet search to find information.

Figure 3.2. Tools for Understanding

Tool	Examples	Description	Literacy Application
Annotate	Google Docs Adobe Scribble Notability	Students would upload or create documents and then annotate these using a tool such as Evernote, which allows you to take notes on digital images, websites, and texts. These notes can be text or audio based.	Have students choose a website, video, or image and record their thinking about this text; then have them share this with the class.
Wiki	PB Works Wikispaces	Wikis are websites where users can add, delete, or edit information. These are great when you want students to create a collaborative text.	Have students jigsaw a text where each group would create a wiki on a different chapter, and then share this chapter with the whole group.
Webquest	Questgarden Zunal Teacherweb	A Webquest is an inquiry-oriented activity in which some or all of the information with which students interact comes from resources on the Internet.	Have students engage in a Webquest on the Common Core State Standards.
Blogging	Blogger	Blogs are essentially online journals that allow you to share your ideas with others and comment.	Have students keep a blog during a class to record what they are learning and thinking as the class progresses.
Timelines	xTimeline Tiki-Toki Dipty	Web-based timelines allow the user to create a chronological order of facts and information. These timelines also allow the user to add visual images, web links, and videos.	Have students create a timeline about the stages of second-language development.
Screen Capture	Jing Screen-cast-o-matic Screenbird Knovio	Screen captures enable the user to record his or her screen. This is great for sharing information with others so they can see what you are seeing on your screen.	Have students record their screens as they are viewing a website and record their thoughts about the site as audio or video.

Figure 3.3. Tools for Applying

Tool	Examples	Description	Literacy Application
Presentation Tools	PowerPoint Keynote Knovio (a tool for enhancing PowerPoint presentations) Prezi	These presentation tools enable the student to share information using text, images, and videos.	Have students make a PowerPoint on a topic such as working with English language learners to improve comprehension.
Blogging	Blogger	Blogs are essentially online journals that allow you to share your ideas with others and comment.	Blogs can be used at different levels. At this level you would ask the students to apply what they are learning as it relates to their own context. This works especially well in practicum settings where students are reflecting upon certain literacy topics as they see them in their classrooms.
Virtual Posters	Glogster.edu	Glogs are online multimedia virtual posters.	Students can create a Glog describing how a unit is taught in their classroom. They can include videos, photos, and links to classroom materials.
Flowcharts	Giffy Mindmeister Mindomo	There are many mind-mapping and chart tools that can be used online. These can be used either collaboratively or individually and then shared with others.	Have students record a conversation in their classroom and then create a discourse map where they visually represent the discussion. Students can then analyze how discussions are conducted in their classrooms and make some recommendations for practice.

Analyzing

When we ask students to analyze we want them to deconstruct knowledge and look at something from its multiple parts. We want students to integrate knowledge into different structures and think critically about issues. We have to be more thoughtful about how we support this level of thinking, as it requires us to construct more detailed tasks in which students can engage (see Figure 3.4).

Evaluating

We want students to be able to make judgments based on logical facts and information. In this stage they are critically thinking about different pieces of information, how they are connected, and how the conclusion is supported by the details. We want them to argue, defend, critique, and

Figure 3.4. Tools for Analyzing

Tool	Examples	Description	Literacy Application
Surveys	Survey Monkey Poll Everywhere Google Forms	Students can create online surveys by creating their own questions, sending the link out to others via email, and collecting data on a topic.	Have students create a survey on a literacy topic and send to others. After they receive the information, have them analyze the data, graph what they learned, and draw conclusions.
Mind Maps	Mindmeister Mindomo	A mind map is a diagram to visually present information in a weblike fashion.	Give students a concept and have them come up with a mind map as they brainstorm the definition of this concept. Then students can analyze one another's mind maps for patterns of similarity and difference.
Mashups	Audacity Mashupcity Pipes	A mashup is a webpage or digital or audio text that is created by combining data, images, text, or audio to create something different. These are most commonly done with music or videos but can be done with visual texts as well.	Create a mashup of a text that you have read by combining audio, video, and text.

judge information. This can be done through debating, discussion, pre-sentation, or validating. At this level, a discussion is usually the best tech-nology tool for supporting this level of thinking (see Figure 3.5).

Creating

This is the highest level of thinking. You are asking students to take information that they have learned and create something new and dif-ferent with it. Students have to synthesize and pull different information into a new form. It is also a way for them to be producers of knowledge and share this with others (see Figure 3.6).

TOOLS THAT SUPPORT SOCIAL LEARNING

Churches (2009) asserts that collaboration is not a 21st-century skill, but rather a 21st-century *essential*. In Chapter 2 we discussed the importance of developing an online learning community, and there are many tech-nology tools that can facilitate this connection. Many of these tools are similar to the tools that support learning and active engagement in course material. While the tools can be the same, it is important that our goals are clear when we choose technology and align it with our objectives. If our objective is to create a learning community (which we argue should be one of your objectives) the tools you choose should help the members of that learning community share ideas with one another and contribute to one another's knowledge growth, and they should help members support collaborative thinking. Supporting social learning is especially important in literacy education. Not only is the pedagogy of literacy education rooted in social constructivist theory, the very root of literacy is communication. Reading, writing, speaking, and listening—all foundations of literacy—are for the purpose of being able to communicate effectively in a variety of settings. Exploring ways to support and enhance communication through technology is especially important in 21st-century literacy education.

A powerful advantage of a learning community is to share ideas. We have found that our students have loved hearing what other teachers do in their classrooms. Each semester in final evaluations, we hear students com-ment on how many ideas and resources they get from fellow classmates. Having students keep blogs, share their social bookmarking sites, create wikis, and make presentations through PowerPoint slide shows, Prezis, and Glogs of their practice fosters a supportive learning community.

We also want our learning communities to support the growth of knowledge. While getting a plethora of new teaching ideas is a wonderful outcome, we also want to push our students to think deeply about literacy

Figure 3.5. Tools for Evaluating

Tool	Examples	Description	Literacy Application
Audio—Asynchronous Discussions	Gong Voice Board WimbaVoice Tools	There are tools that allow for audio discussions to take place. These voice boards can be real time or not depending on your need.	In groups, give students a text and have them analyze it based on qualitative, quantitative, and reader and text factors. Have them defend their thinking through an asynchronous discussion around the text. Each group will then submit their text recommendation to the whole class.
Synchronous Discussions	Talkshoe Go to Meeting Skype Collaborate	These tools allow users to participate in real-time collaborative discussions.	Have the students conduct a "mock" literacy team meeting where they are evaluating and making recommendations about student instruction based on simulated student information. These team meetings can be recorded and summarized offline as well.
Blogging	Blogger Wordpress	Blogs are online journals that allow you to share your ideas with others and comment. They can be used at a variety of levels. At this level of thinking you can use a blog for students to respond to a prompt that asks them to evaluate information.	Assign each student a country and have them compare that country's literacy rate and achievement and compare this to ours. Students will write a blog post about this comparison and engage in a whole-class discussion about recommendations to improve literacy instruction in the United States.

Figure 3.6. Tools for Creating

Tool	Examples	Description	Literacy Application
Videos	Vimeo YouTube Animoto Flixtime	There are many applications that allow you to create your own videos (like Animito or Flixtime) or to upload your own video onto a password-protected server (YouTube or Vimeo).	Have students make videos of themselves teaching a literacy lesson and share this with the class to create a class video notebook of literacy strategies.
Podcasts	Audacity	Students also can create their own podcasts. Podcasts are audio texts that can be listened to through the computer or on a portable Mp3 player or iPad/iPod.	Have each student investigate a literacy issue and create a podcast summarizing what they learned and making recommendations.
Animation	Doink Cartoon Maker Fuzzwich Voki Go!Animate	Animation is similar to movie-making using real or computer-generated images.	Students can create a teaching video on a specific topic. This can be watched by others in the class to communicate new knowledge.
Publishing	Classroom Notes Plus English Journal Language Arts The Reading Teacher Voices from the Middle Talking Points ReadWriteThink	Teachers should see themselves as contributors to the profession. By submitting work to professional journals, we are encouraging them to be active members in these professional communities.	Students can submit original work—either scholarly, like their report on an action research project, or creatively, like a literacy lesson that they created for publication.
Website	Google Sites Webnode Yola SnapPages	A website has multiple webpages that are linked to present information.	Students can create their own websites on the Big Five reading components and add website links, videos, audios, and instructional strategy suggestions. These can be shared with the whole class and can be kept as a resource.

theory and practice. By using technology tools that support asynchronous and synchronous discussions, promote reading blogs, inspire creating meaningful presentations, and facilitate analyzing practice through videos, we can enhance student learning through our online teaching. One tool that we have found particularly helpful is Voice Thread. On a Voice Thread we can take a topic and create a slide with information. Then each member of the community can share his or her perspective on that topic through audio, video, or text. Voice Thread is a wonderful way to bring together a virtual learning community in order to forward thinking on a topic.

Finally, technology can be used to support collaboration. This is especially critical, since most likely all the members of a community will not be in physical proximity. While Skype sessions or threaded discussions are a logical way to communicate at a distance, there are some other tools we can use as well. For example, there are some online brainstorming tools such as Whiteboarding and Scriblink that enable a group to share a blank template and all contribute to this template. Wikis, which are collaborative websites, also offer the opportunity for a group to work together to create a shared text. Students can meet live through tools such as Go to Meeting, Skype, Big Blue Marble, and Collaborate. Finally, Google Docs allows a group to create a single document that is shared between group members, where they can all add and edit. We need to be deliberate in how we use technology to support learning communities. There are many wonderful tools available, and surely more on their way!

SPOTLIGHT: LANE'S MOVE TO INCORPORATING TECHNOLOGY

In my EDU 742 Content Area Literacy class, we spend some time reading and discussing instructional strategies that support students' literacy skills reading nonfiction and content-based texts. Twice in the semester I ask students to take a strategy that they have learned and apply it to their specific setting. The students research, experiment with, and reflect on the strategy and then share this with the class through a strategy demonstration. In the past I had the students share unit plans or lesson plans and perhaps make a PowerPoint presentation. When I moved this assignment online I decided I wanted to pair this assignment with working with more technology tools.

I decided to differentiate the format of these presentations. I provide a list of how the demonstrations can be done and the students choose. I offer choices such as creating a PowerPoint, a Prezi, a Glog, a video, or a photo share (I also give students the option of writing a traditional lesson plan).We do these strategy demonstrations once in the middle of the semester and then again at the end of the semester, and I ask that the students use different formats for their sharing each time. I also provide some exemplars of past projects so that students can have an idea what others have done in the past. While the goal is for students to translate strategies into practice, I also use this assignment to push students to use a technology tool to communicate what they have learned. The sharing of these demonstrations also contributes to building a learning community where the students share these great ideas and learn from one another.

Since I started doing this assignment, my students have created amazing demonstrations of literacy strategies. They have exceeded my expectations for using technology as a tool for learning, and every semester my students rave about how much they learn from one another through this assignment and how excited they are to take these presentation tools into their own classrooms!

CONSIDERATIONS WHEN CHOOSING TOOLS

Since new technologies are constantly changing, the ability to "learn and relearn" is an integral part of being literate in the 21st century. This is a vast deviation from the traditional tenets of literacy that focused on learning a discrete set of skills once and for all. Of critical importance is the decisionmaking required as we use these new technologies as tools for teaching and learning. Moore and Kearsley (2012) assert that "simply making a video podcast presentation or putting lecture PowerPoint material on a website is no more teaching than it would be to send the students a book through the mail" (p. 136). We also need to keep in mind that technology should *never* be the driver of the learning—*you* are the driver and the technology is just the vehicle through which learning is conducted. Whitesel (1998) reminds us that "technology does not teach students; effective teachers do" (p.1).

It is crucial that you think through how you use technology in your online learning environment. First, you need to make sure that your learning objective is driving your choice of technology. You need to ensure that you don't get lost in the flashiness of technology and sacrifice the underlying goal. Technology needs to be accessible and usable to all participants—watch out for the bells and whistles that do nothing to promote and further learning. In addition, you need to consider the ease of using a particular technology. If the tool that you choose requires a huge learning curve, then the time to learn the tool may overshadow its effectiveness as it relates to your objective. Most tools are free or part of a Learning Management System (LMS). However, there are many other tools that have a cost—either to the student or to you—so make sure you research this before you adopt a tool. You also need to consider if you want to use a tool that is internal (part of your LMS—if you use one) or external (outside your LMS). For example, for one class Lane decided to use the wiki that came with her Blackboard LMS. Her students hated it! It was difficult to edit, not easy to import images and text, and hard to find, and it disappeared after the course was over. The next semester she used Wikispaces—an external wiki—which was much easier to use, continued to "live" beyond the course, and was a tool that many of the teachers were familiar with from using it in their own classrooms. Although some students grumbled about having to "leave" the LMS for the course, overall it was a much better fit for her learning objective. Having a quick tools checklist can facilitate choosing what technology tools to include in your teaching (see Figure 3.7).

TENSIONS, RENEGOTIATIONS, AND CRITICAL REFLECTIONS

Choosing the right tools should be a time-consuming part of your role as an instructor but ultimately will reduce the labor intensity of learning and creatively transcend teacher-centered instruction. Using technology as a tool in online learning is a big part of the learning process, but also comes with many questions and considerations. For many of us, getting familiar with these technology tools requires a huge learning curve. In addition to creating powerful objectives, aligning them with learning activities and meaningful assignments, creating a learning community, and communicating our teacher presence, we also have to think through a whole host of technology tools. This can be overwhelming work! There are so many tools out there and the number is growing daily. Keeping up with these

Figure 3.7. Checklist for Choosing Tools

Technology Tool	Yes	No	Notes
Is your intended use of the technology tool aligned with your learning objective?			
Is the tool accessible to all (Mac and PC compatible)?			
Is there a large learning curve associated with the tool?			
Is the tool free?			
Can the tool be used outside a Learning Management System (LMS)?			
Are your students familiar with the tool (or a similar tool)?			
Does the tool have K–12 application?			

tools can feel like a huge task. In addition, our students have a variety of comfort zones around technology—not all online learners are digital "natives" (and when they are, it does not necessarily mean they can navigate all of these tools!). Finding the right balance of time is difficult.

Incorporating technology tools also requires some renegotiations. We need to be aware of how the tools we use position both the students and us—the teachers—in relation to teaching and learning. We have to make sure that we assert ourselves front and center of the learning and not get overshadowed by the glitz and glamour of the tools. Furthermore, we need to consider how the incorporation of these tools impacts our identities as teachers and learners ourselves. For some of us, using technology in this way is quite different from how we learned and it changes how we envisioned our teaching and learning would look.

Finally, the explosion of technology tools has been rapid. We are still in the beginning stages of trying out these tools and seeing what they can do, but we cannot lose sight of linking these tools to learning. We need to engage in critical analysis and research around using these tools. We need to ask ourselves: What tools best correlate to learning effectiveness? How can tools be integrated in the most beneficial fashion? Is there a saturation point for tool integration—and if so, what is it? By asking these questions we will ensure that the incorporation of technology as tools will promote active, constructive, and social learning and empower us as teachers and support our students in engaging in literacy practices in new and transformative ways.

Activities to Try

- Pick one technology tool from each level of Bloom's Digital Technology pyramid and try to develop an assignment around this tool.
- Learn about a new tool that you have not used before.
- Do a survey with your students to see what technology tools they already use in their classrooms.
- Go through the tool checklist with some tools that you currently use.

VOICES FROM THE FIELD

In my years of experience, I have learned that effective online course design requires more than knowledge about elements of strong design. It requires time, experimentation, creativity, and purpose. As I worked to develop an online program from the ground up, I learned that the process not only takes more time than expected, but also takes unexpected uses of time. Specifically, I've learned a lot about making time to interact effectively online. One way I've done this is to incorporate protocols (McDonald, Zydney, Dichter, & McDonald, 2012) into my online discussions. Protocols encourage participation among all class members, can allow for multiple modes of participation, and can also stimulate deep thinking about important ideas. For me, this meant a shift in my teaching toward more heavily student-led discussions. The fact that this discussion strategy was not only new for me, but often for my students as well, led to new design decisions on my part.

Even with a background in Instructional Design and Technology (IDT), I find that there is always so much to learn and that change is a part of our role as online educators and learners. It is my belief that effective course design does not only come from theory, but requires a schema from which to work. In other words, without doing "it," one cannot truly understand the dynamic complexity that is online teaching and learning. Changes to my online discussions came only after I had experienced online discussions that fell flat. And while these discussions provided ways to build community and interact with content, they were also—at the core— issues of instructional design. This is not all that different from my face-to-face teaching in many aspects. Adapting my work in either direction (from F2F to online, or vice versa) requires thoughtful mapping and adaptation. I do believe technology has played a significant role in my ability to create engagement experiences for my students—and to design my courses accordingly—no matter the setting.

—Suzanne Ehrlich, field service assistant professor,
Signed Language Interpreting and Deaf Studies, University of Cincinnati

CHAPTER 4

Designing Effective Learning Experiences

> **Questions to Ponder**
>
> - What are/were your fears/uncertainties about teaching online?
> - In your opinion, what are the essential elements of an online course?
> - How does your philosophy of learning drive your teaching?
> - How do you align your objectives with activities and assessment?

When you think about a college classroom you might picture a lecture hall with lots of students squeezed into wooden chairs—or you might picture students sitting around a large table with swivel chairs, or perhaps sitting in groups with tables facing the front of the room. These are images that many of us conjure when we think about our higher educational experiences. Perhaps the space may be different but two things were constant—there was always a teacher at the head of the class (or seated beside us) and other students surrounding us. This was the model that most of us experienced, that our parents experienced, and that their parents experienced.

Now think about a different learning environment—perhaps you are in your bathrobe, or at a coffee shop, or in a library sitting by yourself. You might be working in the middle of the night or between breaks at your job. You might never have spoken to or smiled at your teacher and never laid eyes on your classmates. Your classmates may be from the next town or perhaps half a world away. This is a new vision of learning that our parents and grandparents could never even have imagined and perhaps one that seems at odds with the experiences we had in school. However, this is a new model of education and one that is changing the way we approach teaching and learning. With this shift in paradigm of learning we also need to shift our approaches to constructing learning spaces within this new educational context.

Taking our traditional visions of learning and translating them into a new way of configuring learning experiences in a digital age may seem like a daunting task. However, one need not think of the process as the proverbial "throwing out the baby with the bathwater." Instead, this is a wonderful opportunity to push ourselves to think deeply about pedagogy and how we learn. It is an opportunity to facilitate a heightened awareness of our teaching and to reconfigure how we perceive learning without the boundaries of space and time. It is also an opportunity to challenge ourselves to understand the foundation of learning and how we can create new pedagogical approaches that are rooted in what we know works best.

Creating online learning experiences can be challenging, stimulating, exciting, and transformative. In the previous chapters we advocated for the primacy of the teacher, the need to build learning communities, and the importance of using technology as a tool to enhance learning. In this chapter we will take you through the process of designing an online learning experience. You will see many familiar pieces of creating a learning environment that transcend this new teaching environment—but you will also be asked to think about how these approaches are altered in an online setting. Moving education online can be an empowering but also daunting process. When we leave behind those physical spaces—including the creaky wooden desks and overhead projectors—we undertake an exciting opportunity to put pedagogy under the lens and at the same time challenge ourselves to engage differently in this new world of online learning.

Many of us are eager to jump into online learning and many of us have made the leap already and are looking for ways to improve our practice. However, one thing that we all have in common is that we all want to be the best teachers that we can be regardless of the medium through which we teach. To be an effective online teacher you need many skills—luckily most of these skills are ones that you have already developed as a face-to-face teacher. Teaching online is a shift in our existing practices—we are using the same teaching tools, just applying them in a different context. For some this is a scary shift, and there are many questions and concerns that go along with teaching online. For others this presents a new challenge.

While these fears are certainly reasonable ones, and something that many of us who jumped into the online teaching world have experienced, there are also many benefits of taking our teaching practices into a new context. Teaching online forces us to closely examine how we teach and why we teach the way we do. In this chapter, we take apart the design process and focus on what good pedagogy looks like in an online environment (and, not surprisingly, this is not different from what good pedagogy looks like in a traditional setting). Bennett and Lockyer (2004) believe that online teaching can lead to a new level of complexity in our teaching, one that gives us freedom "to design a schedule that is tailored more appropriately to the subject activities rather than organized around regularly timetabled meetings" (p. 237). One huge benefit of online learning is that it is not bound by time or space—it does not have to abide by the constraints of the once-a-week meeting; it is more fluid and therefore has the potential to be more transformative.

DESIGNING AN ONLINE LEARNING EXPERIENCE

While the steps in creating an online learning experience are basically the same as a face-to-face class, it is important not to just replicate each step. It is best not to just move what you have done previously for traditional classes over to an online environment. While the steps are the same, the medium is different; as a result, you will need to consider how taking learning online changes the paradigm for learning.

In the next part of the chapter we will take you through the steps of creating a successful learning experience in an online setting. One big difference between face-to-face instruction and online instruction is the front-loading of course design. Much of the work in designing and teaching an online class is done before the course even begins. While this can also be true of face-to-face classes, preplanning is of particular importance in online courses.

To illustrate this point, let's consider just one aspect of course design: the first day of class. In a face-to-face class, it is quite typical to spend much of that first meeting sharing information about how the class will unfold over time. The instructor very often walks students through the syllabus, and in so doing highlights certain points, adds information that inadvertently may have been excluded, and answers students' questions about the course. As you think about this scenario and your own experiences in this regard, think about how much information is conveyed through the student-teacher interaction—especially information that is needed by students but only conveyed after students express these needs, either verbally or through facial expressions and body language. The first day of class is almost always a time to expand upon and clarify the information that the instructor had planned to share. In other words, the plan provides a strong base but in itself does not carry the introduction to the course. Further, consider how much information will be conveyed in the coming weeks, as students bring more questions and the instructor thinks of more information that students should have. In fact, at the end of each class meeting, the instructor may think of several items she wishes she had mentioned, and will jot down notes so as to remember to share them the next time. Similarly, students will think of questions they wished they had asked and will bring those questions to the next class meeting. If there is an urgent matter, the instructor and students may correspond online between class meetings, but otherwise both parties are secure in the knowledge that they will see each other again soon, discussing more and more each time.

Now think about the first day of an online class. Students will access the class at different points throughout the day, and their interactions with the syllabus and other course materials will be done on their own. If the syllabus is the only item available, it may raise as many questions as it answers regarding course content and expectations. While a good online course is always interactive, opportunities for the instructor to expand upon and clarify ideas, based on student questions and conversation, will very rarely be "just in time" as they are during the initial course meeting of a face-to-face class. Additionally, students will explore the class site in individualistic, non-linear ways. Some will explore information about assignments first. Others will look for the readings that have been posted. And others will want to look for links to resources such as IT assistance, the university library, or general university policies. This is one reason why anticipating questions and thoughtfully considering how much information to provide, and at which points to provide it, takes on unique importance online. Any information that is provided online should be provided with enough detail so as to truly be informative rather than merely question generating. This does not mean that everything about a course needs to be provided during the first week, but it does mean details that are not provided but that students are likely to inquire about must be addressed. Statements such as "The rubric for this assignment will be available soon," or "Look for your first reflection journal prompt at the beginning Week 2" are simple ways to address likely student questions. This is also why it makes sense to decide in advance whether there is an order in which you suggest students explore the course site, and if so, that this is made clear. One way to do this is to label the first tab on your course site "Start Here." It is also important to run a test on each link you include on your course site. Either you or someone else should click on each item on your site as it is posted to be sure it opens and is accessible, whether it is a PDF file, a video file, or a hyperlink. This is also why the time spent designing the class as a learning community (see Chapter 2 for more details) and appropriating technology tools to support active, constructive, social learning (see Chapter 3) is time well spent. Students who work in community can often address one another's questions, and when students and the instructor are in community together, there is an easier exchange of information (especially in the absence of shared physical space) than when students perceive themselves as working through a course alone, in an unconnected way. If a course is well thought out and planned ahead of time, then once the class begins the instructor can focus on teaching and the students can focus on learning, rather than focusing on the tools and logistics needed to do each of these.

While some of us may have instructional designers to work with as we take our teaching online, it is important to remember that you (the literacy teacher educator) need to be in the driver's seat of the design. The instructional designer can help you with logistics and technology, but you need to control the content and how it is best delivered. While collaboration can lead to more effective learning designs, most likely your instructional designer will not be a literacy expert. A good working team will lead to the creation of a wonderful online experience, but the more you are informed about course design, the more control you will have in designing an effective online learning experience.

Step One: Learning Theory

The way we construct educational experiences is directly related to the theory of learning to which we subscribe. As mentioned previously in Chapter 2, teacher education tends to be rooted in a social constructivist learning approach. This approach asserts that learning takes place through the dynamic interchange between the content and the social situations that support this content. In a very basic sense Dewey (1916) described education as occurring when individuals interact with their learning environment. Learning is not a one-dimensional activity that takes place between the learner and the content. Most teacher education courses and professional learning experiences are not based on the lecture model, but rather on the principles of dynamic interchange, where a learning community is created and through this community members collaboratively exchange ideas, reflect on these ideas, and engage in creating new knowledge (this was explored in greater depth in Chapter 2).

Since learning is rooted in the social construction of knowledge, there are some key elements that drive the creation of effective learning environments—both in face-to-face learning and online learning. As explored in Chapter 1, these elements include creating learning experiences that are motivating, student-centered, support student involvement, establish high expectations, and promote connectedness. Articulating these key elements is crucial regardless of the learning environment you use—however, one danger of online teaching is that the learning environment can easily overshadow the rationale behind it. For example, it is easy to get lost in the technology tools, or the challenges of face-to-face contact, or the creation of dynamic multimedia materials, and lose sight of the role that all of these play in the creation of a social constructivist learning experience.

Regardless of what type of online learning experience that you are creating—perhaps it is a completely online course, or a blended/hybrid course (part online and part face-to-face), or a professional development opportunity—you need to be aware of how your perspective of learning shapes how you create this environment. We want these online experiences to reflect the belief that learners gain new knowledge through exploring, manipulating, creating, sharing, and discovering with others.

Our belief in literacy as a social practice is articulated in the following principles that drive our creation of online learning experiences. You will see these beliefs woven through the learning activities we create, the assignments we give, and the learning community we develop. The first principle is the primacy of creating a learning community. Swan and Shea (2005) assert, "Knowledge is inseparable from practice and practice is inseparable from the communities in which it occurs" (p. 241). We believe in collaborative social experiences, and the creation of these learning communities is at the heart of all of our online courses (see Chapter 2). Second, learning should be student centered. Learning should focus on the learners—not on you, the teacher! You may be able to dazzle your audience with your ability to make MTV-quality videos, but if this is disconnected from the learner's ability to engage in the material then it is not an effective practice. We also need students to engage in learning actively; they need to be given opportunities to read, speak, listen, write, and demonstrate in different ways so that they are actively involved in their learning. Distance education is not passive! For learning to occur you cannot just sit there and read or listen—a student has to be involved and take an active learning stance. Next, you need to ensure dynamic interchanges between the teacher and students. Teachers must be present in all learning activities—not just create the course and then disappear. For effective online learning to take place, there needs to be a human being on the other side of the computer, and the students need to know this! It is the teacher who facilitates a social constructivist space, and this must be reflected in the course design. Finally, it is important to present stimulating content. Learning arises from multiple opportunities for reflection, integration of ideas, creation of new knowledge, and challenging experiences. Since we believe in active learning we must present content with which our students want to engage.

Step Two: Choosing Goals and Objectives

Once we articulate our theoretical approach that drives the creation of our instructional choices, we next need to align this with learning goals and objectives. In teacher education, we want our teachers to be reflective and critical thinkers. We want our students to develop a repertoire of strategies and approaches, based in theory and research that they can draw upon to meet the needs of their students (see Chapter 5 for more on the standards that drive our objectives).

While we all develop learning goals when creating a learning environment, it is especially important in an online setting that the goals are clear and restated frequently. This repetition is especially important in the course design process as it is the goals that drive course development. It is equally important for goals to be clear for the students since you are not physically present to interpret, elaborate, or explain these goals. Furthermore, clarifying goals helps students establish the learning frame upon which the activities and assessments are connected. In keeping with our learning philosophy, we want our goals to reflect the higher-level thinking and engagement that we hope to promote, such as having students evaluate, compare and contrast, analyze, synthesize, examine, criticize, and diagnose.

In an online course you may break these down into *course goals*, *module objectives*, and *learning outcomes*.

- *Course Goals:* These are the overarching goals that you hope the learning experiences in your course will accomplish. There should not be too many of these—the module objectives upon which these are based are the opportunity to articulate specificity of each of these goals. For example, Lane is responsible for five literacy courses in a master's concentration. It is important that the overall goals for each course align with one another as well as with the IRA Standards upon which all of the courses are based. The course goals are broad and ensure that the students are developing the global competencies that they need to be effective literacy teachers. For example, one of the overall goals is, *"Students will be able to examine, create, evaluate, and reflect on a variety of literacy assessments as they are directly connected to data-driven instruction and student literacy achievement."*
- *Module Objectives:* Once you have set the overarching course goals, you need to develop learning objectives for each module or chunk of learning. The module objectives are more concrete and stated in learner-centered language. Just like the course goals, the module objectives need to be written for a variety of knowledge levels. In Lane's Literacy Assessment as Teaching Tools course, an objective may be, *"Teachers will apply their understanding of literacy assessment in developing a literacy assessment plan for an individual student."* Learning objectives should appear in numerous places both so that they are clear to the students and so that students are aware of what they can expect to learn as a result of engaging in specific learning experiences and course assignments. For example, learning objectives can be placed in an alignment table in the syllabus, at the beginning of each module, and at the top of each assignment description.
- *Learning Outcomes:* Sometimes it is helpful to break down goals and objectives even further to learning outcomes. Outcomes

are what you hope students will know and/or be able to do by the end of the course or at the end of a particular learning experience. The desired learning outcomes need to be clear to the student as well as concise. The learning outcome for the goal listed above would be, "*Students will demonstrate their ability to conduct an informal reading inventory on one student and use that information to plan related instruction.*"

Step Three: Learning Activities

The learning activities provide a bridge between the learning objectives and the assessments. Students should see a clear connection between these two and also fully understand how engaging in these activities will help them meet these objectives. These activities are also a way to get the students to be actively involved with the content. Think of these learning activities as what happens during face-to-face class time or a meeting.

In terms of learning activities, many online and hybrid courses use the Quality Matters (QM) rubric to help them design and assess their course. Quality Matters is a faculty-centered peer review process with the goal of promoting quality learning experiences for students. Quality Matters states that "Instructional materials [should be] sufficiently comprehensive to achieve stated course objectives and learning outcomes and are prepared by qualified persons [who are] competent in their fields." We would add that the resources should also be varied in order to keep student attention, and also represent a range of perspectives. Also, we believe that it is important to provide varied activities and a range of representation of material so that we can meet the needs of a variety of learners. In addition, in education the landscape is always changing. Since we started teaching literacy methods courses we have had to incorporate information from the National Reading Panel (National Institute of Child Health and Human Development, 2000), information about response to intervention, and now the Common Core State Standards, to name a few. Because things change so rapidly, it is really not possible to make a course and then just reuse it over and over. Spending time looking for new materials and new information is part of an online educator's responsibilities. Reviewing current texts and incorporating articles from journals to supplement instructional materials is necessary to keep materials current and relevant.

Step Four: Choosing Assignments

The assignments that we give are based on the learning objectives and are supported through the learning activities. The assignments give the students the opportunity to demonstrate their learning. One thing that is different when creating assignments in an online environment is to really think through how the assignments capture the unique strengths of a digital learning platform. It is important to create meaningful assignments that play upon the delivery system and also capture your philosophy of learning. Powerful assignments engage students, connect to their lives, and push them to think differently and critically about issues around literacy. We can avoid the "show-and-tell" types of assignments by carefully considering the assignments that will stimulate deeper thinking and engagement.

Assignments are also powerful when we ask students to engage in reflective activities. For example, Lee (2009) found that the most effective assignments in teacher education were those that allowed them to connect to field experiences (i.e., portfolios, critical reflections, and observations), provided them with opportunities to video their teaching for analysis, demonstrated methods for engaging students, and promoted reflective thinking. The assignments that were least effective were tests, quizzes, and weekly reportings. Marsh, Lammers, and Alvermann (2012) assert that online participants need to be analyzing, synthesizing, and evaluating, and this can be done through online discussions and carefully planned assignments. This can be tricky in an online class, as we often look for ways to know that our students are present. Sometimes we fall into the trap of assigning lots of busywork in the name of making sure that they are engaged. Providing fewer, deeper assignments is more effective than lots of "check-in" assignments (see Appendix A for many sample assignments from our courses).

In addition, it is important to vary assignments—students need multiple ways to demonstrate that they are learning and can communicate the information. It is also important that we use exemplars when appropriate. There are many online tools that allow us to provide annotated examples. Assignments that offer choices and are based on student interactivity are what we are striving for when we match assignments to our learning activities and course goals. All of these principles are part of a Universal Design for Learning (UDL) approach, as well as good practice in any setting.

SPOTLIGHT: LANE'S PROFESSIONAL LITERACY LESSON PLANS

One very typical assignment that many teacher educators have used is to have their teachers create lesson plans. In the past I have had students create these lessons based on either a similar lesson plan, a lesson plan template from their schools, or criteria given to them by me that I wanted to make sure they included. Sometimes I would give them a topic (such as, "Everyone write a vocabulary lesson"), or give them a choice (e.g., "Pick one of the big five reading components"). The students would write their lessons and share them with me and perhaps with the class. While my students were doing good work, I realized that I was just promoting show-and-tell type of activities that were not meeting my goal of pushing my students to be more engaged teacher-scholars who work in a learning community. After reflecting on my philosophy of learning and the strengths of online learning I refreshed this assignment to create a new and improved lesson plan activity.

I believe that being part of a virtual learning community will be increasingly important to teachers, given the power of technology and also the lack of professional development budgets. I started to think about the online communities that I value and I thought about the power of online lesson sharing. I use ReadWriteThink (RWT) most commonly (a joint IRA/NCTE/Thinkfinity website). RWT provides high-quality literacy resources, lessons, materials, and units through a peer-reviewed process. All lessons are based on the theory-to-practice model and are rigorous and in-depth. I have gone to RWT countless times to look for lesson inspiration or resources, and this led me to think about changing my lesson plan assignment to mirror the process that RWT uses to vet its lesson plans. My new lesson plan assignment (creatively called Professional Literacy Lesson Plan) uses RWT as its inspiration and model. It captures my goals of supporting students who are actively engaging with technology, being part of a learning community, and pushing themselves to think more deeply about literacy instruction.

For this new assignment students write a lesson based on the components of a ReadWriteThink lesson plan. Students go through a review process with this lesson, as if they were submitting this lesson to RWT, to help push them to think more in depth about literacy instruction. Students use a lesson plan template and submission guidelines to drive this work. ReadWriteThink is a powerful professional community that provides high-quality literacy materials; this assignment emulated this process, and in doing so students engaged in a similar collaborative process. Students worked in groups and at the end of the class each group submitted one lesson (the best) to be reviewed by the whole class. Then the whole class evaluated the top lessons and chose one lesson from this review process to actually be submitted to RWT.

The students loved the new, improved lesson plan. One student commented, "I liked the opportunity to write a lesson plan and share that lesson plan with group members. It provided an opportunity to get feedback, which is something that you do not necessarily often have when in your classroom."

ASSESSING ASSIGNMENTS

In a face-to-face environment you can give an assignment and then explain it to the students. By contrast, in an online space it is really important that you are very thorough with your assignment descriptions. Establishing clear expectations for assignments is one of the most important things you can do as an online teacher. It is important to spend extra time up front explaining what students are to do and how they will be evaluated. Many times you can take some time to explain assignments—either synchronously or asynchronously. However, frequently students access these assignments on their own and often without your presence, so you need to be careful to be clear right from the start.

Your assignments also need to be clearly aligned with course goals and learning objectives. They should flow from the learning activities and students should see these as natural next steps from the learning activities. One thing you can do is to create an assignment description guide for each assignment. This description could have the following parts:

- *Learning Objective*: What objective does this assignment connect to? Make sure that your assignments are hitting those upper levels of Bloom's taxonomy.
- *Assignment Description*: What is the purpose of this assignment? Give a brief explanation of what the students are supposed to do.
- *Task Description*: What steps need to be taken to complete this assignment? These can be bulleted or numbered for clarity.
- *Rubric for Grading Expectation*: Developing clear rubrics is helpful in order to establish clear expectations and also to assist you while grading.

It is important to give students specific feedback on their assignments. Remember, they are not physically seeing you, so one way to develop your teacher presence is through giving feedback and comments on assignments. There are many ways to do this. You can use the rubric as a place to give comments. Also, many Learning Management Systems (LMS) provide a place in a grade book to leave comments. One thing you can also use is the track changes function in Microsoft Word. When students submit assignments, have them submit these in a Word document, then save that document to your desktop. Use "track changes" to leave sidebar comments or make editorial insertions, and then resave the document and send it back to the student. Some students like to see comments woven through their document as opposed to just one comment at the end. It also lets them know that you have read their whole assignment! Another thing you can do is to use Jing (www.techsmith.com/jing.html)

or Screencast-o-matic (www.screencastomatic.com) to leave audio (and even video) feedback on students' work. You can look at their work and simultaneously talk through the work and then send them a link so they can see/hear your feedback. This is especially good to use when you are reviewing multimedia assignments and is a great way to make your teacher presence felt while at the same time providing meaningful feedback.

ROLE OF THE STUDENT

Since most of us have been students for over half of our lives, we pretty much have the schema for what a good student looks like. We know to face our teacher—or the person speaking. We know the importance of eye contact and head nodding. We know how to look engaged (even when we are not) and to raise our hands or wait for the appropriate time to talk. The role of a student is pretty well-established in a face-to-face learning environment. This is not the case when we move learning online. Many of us who teach online may never have been an online student. Because of this we need to be explicit with our students about what it means to be an online student. We need to help them develop the schema that will make them successful.

One way we can help our students is to establish clear expectations for students' roles up front. It is best if this is done up front in the syllabus, introductory material, or the first module. Taking time to communicate your expectations or define what it would mean to be a successful student in this setting is crucial to student success. For example, a list of student expectations could look like this:

- Maintain a high level of professionalism and integrity when participating in any interaction with classmates or the instructor. Please review the principles of "Netiquette" listed in the Getting Started Module. It is important that we carefully consider how we engage with classmates through written expression, as this can be interpreted differently without visual cues.
- Submit quality work that represents your best effort.
- Ask questions when you are not sure of something. I cannot see if you are confused or puzzled. In an online class you must take the opportunity to contact me with questions or comments.
- Check into class at least once a day. This does not necessarily mean spend hours a day in class, but you should commit to at least a daily check-in to stay on top of announcements and discussions. It is also helpful to develop a consistent pattern of working online—it is easy to get behind very quickly.

- Be mindful of your classmates and work productively in your group: Different classmates have different work habits, times online, and schedules. This can get tricky when working in an online group. Communicating your work habits up front with your group will help your group function better.

We can also provide frequent opportunities for self-reflection about student role: This can be done through formative or summative assessments. It can also be built into assignments. Asking students to think about their role in the online environment will help them become more aware of their own learning. Here are some questions you could ask:

- How am I engaging with this content?
- Am I checking in enough?
- Am I being an active learner? If so, how? If not, how can I change this?
- How am I contributing to my learning community (small group/ whole class)?
- What factors are influencing my participation?

Finally, we can support students by providing exemplars or models: This can be done by presenting profiles of online student behaviors, checklists, or engaging in a virtual fishbowl discussion based on a positive and/or negative role model example.

ROLE OF THE INSTRUCTOR

In Chapter 1, we highlighted the importance of the teacher. We feel that it is important to reiterate the key role that the instructor plays in any online learning experience. The National Education Association (NEA) asserts in its Guide to Teaching Online Courses that even with the proliferation of online learning opportunities, all good courses—regardless of how they are delivered—need good teachers. They state, "By definition, online teaching should be done at a distance: however, it should not be conducted in isolation" (2002, p. 8). Furthermore, they continue, "As with any educational innovation, teachers are at the core of online learning" (p. 9).

When we design online learning experiences we need to carefully consider our role in facilitating learning. One way to think about the instructor's role is by acknowledging that instructors should embody *teacher*, *social*, and *cognitive* presence during the course (Garrison, Anderson, & Archer, 2000). It is important to communicate your *teaching presence*.

Teaching presence is fostering a personal connection through the modeling and facilitating of learning. Will you log in multiple times a week, daily, or several times a day? Students should know what your teaching presence style is, since they do not see you in person or have an expectation for when they will see you (whereas in face-to-face classes there is always the minimal expectation of when you will see your teacher). It is also important to communicate your presence because many online instructors have very different approaches to teacher presence. For example, a list of teacher expectations could look like the following:

- I will maintain a positive learning environment for all students.
- I will provide feedback on assignments as quickly as possible—I will use track changes or screen capture to give feedback right in your assignment. Sometimes this takes a bit of time, but I am committed to returning all assignments within the week that they are due.
- I will check emails every day except Saturdays and will respond to students within 24 hours. I usually check in once during the workday and then once in the evening. I do try to turn off my computer after 10 p.m. EST. So if you send me something at night I may not respond immediately.
- I will read all of your online discussions—I may not participate in all of your discussions but will participate when appropriate or necessary.
- I will check Virtual Office and Water Cooler daily.
- I will send out a Sunday announcement to summarize what needs to be done for the upcoming week. I will also send out a midweek check-in announcement with information related to the course.
- Any time my schedule changes I will let you know.

It is also important that we communicate a *social presence*. Social presence is fostering meaningful relationships by establishing a social connection, supporting group cohesion, and making personal connections. Some of this can be done through announcements or emails. Students want to know you care about their learning. Learning online has the potential to be distant. The term "Distance Learning" comes from the fact that the teacher and student are at a physical distance—however, that does not mean there has to be a social distance. We can still be socially present through the interactions that we have with our students—in terms of the content and also with regard to connecting with them on a personal level. Richardson and Swan (2003) found a correlation between social presence, student learning, and course satisfaction. You must actively think about how you are going to communicate your social presence. It is crucial to make students feel welcomed into the learning community. By communicating your social presence, you will help students feel more connected.

Finally, the teacher also has a responsibility to guide the learning process through communicating a *cognitive presence*. Cognitive presence includes designing tasks that increase in cognitive complexity, asking questions that push students' thinking forward, and challenging and triggering student thinking through purposeful activities. We need to demonstrate how we support the cognitive engagement of our students. Our course design and activities create a learning community that is intellectually engaging and that inspires critical thinking. We want our students to get to know us, but most important, we want our students to learn.

TENSIONS, RENEGOTIATIONS, AND CRITICAL REFLECTION

By understanding the elements of course design we can have control over how these online learning experiences are structured. While there are a lot of books out there on designing online courses, there has not been much on how to translate this into discipline-specific content. The following chapters provide a more in-depth look at online learning within the discipline of literacy teacher education. We hope this chapter has helped you think through the various design elements as well as think about some practical applications through sharing pieces of our courses. We still have a lot to learn about designing effective online learning. For example, we would like to know more about how we evaluate teaching and learning online. We also want to know which design elements are most connected to learning and how this is similar to or different from face-to-face teaching. In addition, we want to find better ways to share literacy-related assignments and activities so that we can build a stronger base of collaboration and common experience for our students. We hope that others will continue writing, researching, and sharing best practices as we continue to grow our online teaching pedagogy.

Activities to Try

- Think about the learning theory that drives your instruction. How is this reflected in your course design? Is it clear to you? Is it clear to the students?
- Examine your overall goals, weekly learning objectives, and learning outcomes—are they aligned? Can you make a chart displaying this alignment?
- Update one of your learning activities.
- Look at the sample assignments in Appendix A—do any of them inspire you to update, revise, or try a new assignment?
- Think about how you assess assignments. Is this clear for the students? Can you provide some illustrative exemplars?
- Think about what you expect of your students—draft a list that you can share.
- Think about how you interact in an online environment—draft a list that you can share.

VOICES FROM THE FIELD

Webinars, blogs, apps . . . oh my! In this digital age, literacy educators are frequently exploring new ways of effectively utilizing technology-based learning tools. While the focus of their work is often centered on how to integrate technology into ongoing instruction in the most effective ways, educators are only beginning to scratch the surface of how technology will contribute to their own professional learning. The advent of online courses, webinars, blogs, electronic toolkits, apps, and streaming videos is most likely just the beginning of what is to come.

At the Maine Department of Education, we have seen technology-based professional learning opportunities as an advantageous way to promote literacy learning. The use of increasingly sophisticated webpages designed to put information at the fingertips of educators has become an important vehicle for linking literacy teachers to resources. Additionally, professional learning initiatives like the Cross Discipline Literacy Network and the Literacy for ME initiative both utilize live and archived webinars, streaming video clips, electronic toolkits, and networking platforms as tools for providing literacy-related professional development. Further, literacy micro-courses have been developed and posted online for use by individual educators or professional learning communities to expand their knowledge. Micro-courses provide a self-guided structure that intermixes text reading with live links to Internet-based resources such as video clips, articles, and websites.

While online learning can both enrich and multiply the number of available professional learning resources, it is not without its challenges. The vast array of digital resources leads to the question of quality—just as educators have to teach their students to be savvy Internet consumers, they themselves must learn how to judge the research base of online learning resources to make wise choices, and to connect practical instructional strategies with well-established learning theories and learning standards. Finally, while online learning opportunities can save time in terms of travel and in-person meetings, researching and exploring the plethora of technology-based resources can be extremely time-consuming. Important future considerations will be the development of guidance for how to quickly determine the reliability of online resources, as well as methods for maximizing online learning within reasonable amounts of professional development time.

—Lee Anne Larsen,
literacy specialist, Maine Department of Education

CHAPTER 5

Supporting Critical Learning Outcomes for Reading Professionals

Questions to Ponder

- What role do various sets of standards play in your course design and instruction?
- In your courses, what would you consider to be the central competencies and core knowledge for students to acquire?
- Based on feedback you have received from outside reviews of your teaching (e.g., peer observation) or external program reviews, what are some areas in which you would like to improve your practice?
- In what ways does your use of technology serve as a model for how your students might approach technology integration in their own K-12 settings?

At this point in the book, we hope you are building on your comfort and expertise related to some of the tools, techniques, and understandings related to distance education. In the previous chapters, we have discussed our online identities, ways to build effective online learning communities, and tools that support active, constructive, and social learning. What we have not yet overtly addressed are the ways in which the unique content of our instruction, as literacy teacher educators, impacts and is impacted by the online space within which teaching and learning occur. Whereas key features of online teaching and learning were detailed in the earlier chapters, our goal in this chapter is to foreground the ways in which literacy pedagogy drives the decisions we make and the content that we present.

Teacher education programs in literacy are often aligned with the International Reading Association's (IRA) Standards for Reading Professionals (IRA, 2010), and many are accredited by the Interstate Teacher Assessment and Support Consortium (InTASC), the National Council for Accreditation in Teacher Education (NCATE), the Teacher Education Accreditation Council (TEAC), or the newly formed Council for the Accreditation of Educational Professionals (CAEP), which is a consolidation of

NCATE and TEAC. Further, the International Society for Technology in Education (ISTE, 2012) has developed standards for teachers that highlight the knowledge, skills, and behaviors needed to "teach, work, and learn in an increasingly connected global and digital society." Though not directly linked to accrediting bodies, the competency domains identified in these standards are increasingly reflected in state and national accreditation standards. Further, the most recent InTASC Model Core Teaching Standards (Council of Chief State School Officers, 2011) highlight a shift, also evident in other sets of standards, from a focus on teacher preparation and beginning teachers to an emphasis on the continuum of teacher learning across the career span. This shift is aligned with our focus throughout this book on teacher education and professional practice. In this chapter, we extend our earlier conversations to address the disciplinary focus of our instruction by considering what IRA refers to as the various types of knowledge, skills, and dispositions we aim to cultivate among our students. The InTASC Model Core Teaching Standards (Council of Chief State School Officers, 2011) call these three areas *essential knowledge, performances,* and *critical dispositions.*

CONSIDERING THE STANDARDS THAT GUIDE OUR PRACTICE

In Figure 5.1, we present an overview of the sets of standards that provide the foundation for this chapter, including standards for teacher education and standards for K–12 education. The first set of standards are those to which we, as literacy teacher educators, are held, and they can help guide our course design and instructional practices. The second set of standards are those to which our students will be held when they apply what they've learned in our courses to their work with children and adolescents, and these standards provide another set of guideposts for our instructional decisionmaking. Since our ultimate goal is to foster teacher and student success in the K–12 arena, it is important that our work be aligned with both sets of standards.

Figure 5.1 illustrates the ways in which the standards differ in focus as well as commonalities among them. Increasingly, standards such as these lend structure to our work by focusing our attention equally on what it is we hope our students will learn from our classes and what it is they will do to apply what they learn to their own teaching in K–12 settings. Increasingly, excellence in teacher education is determined by the degree to which students in graduate courses and professional development workshops are able to take what they learn to transform their practice in ways that produce high levels of achievement among their students (Council of Chief State School Officers, 2011).

Figure 5.1. Summary of Standards Documents Addressing Teacher Education and Professional Practice

Standards Document	Stated Emphasis	Key Features
STANDARD OF PRACTICE FOR K–12 TEACHERS		
InTASC Model Core Teaching Standards (Council of Chief School State Officers, 2011)	"the common principles and foundations of teaching practice that cut across all subject areas and grade levels and that are necessary to improve student achievement" (p. 3)	Ten standards grouped into four general teaching categories: The Learner and Learning, Content, Instructional Practice, and Professional Responsibility
IRA Standards for Reading Professionals (IRA, 2010)	"the criteria for developing and evaluating preparation programs for reading professionals . . . [based on a description of] what candidates for the reading profession should know and be able to do in professional settings" (p. 1)	Six overarching standards, each with 3–4 more specific elements underneath; overarching standards: Foundational Knowledge, Curriculum and Instruction, Assessment and Evaluation, Diversity, Literate Environment, Professional Learning and Leadership
International Society for Technology in Education Standards for Teachers (ISTE-T) (ISTE, 2012)	"the standards for evaluating the skills and knowledge educators need to teach, work, and learn in an increasingly connected global and digital society"	Five standards focused on Student Learning and Creativity, Designing and Modeling of Digital Age Learning Experiences and Assessments, Promoting Digital Citizenship, Promoting Professional Growth and Responsibility
STANDARD OF PRACTICE FOR K–12 STUDENTS		
IRA/NCTE Standards for the English Language Arts (IRA/NCTE, 1996)	"defines what students should know about language and be able to do with language" (p. 1)	Twelve standards focusing on experience with a wide range of print and nonprint texts; application of a range of strategies for reading comprehension, interpretation, evaluation, and appreciation as well as writing; adjustment of language use according to purpose and audience; research and synthesis across a variety of sources and media; appreciation of diversity; reflection and critical thinking
Common Core State Standards for the English Language Arts (CCSS) (2010)	College and career readiness and literacy skills needed in the 21st century	Standards in the strands of Reading, Writing, Speaking and Listening, and Language that are tied to College and Career Readiness Anchor Standards in each of these areas
International Society for Technology in Education Standards for Students (ISTE-S) (ISTE, 2012)	"the skills and knowledge students need to learn effectively and live productively in an increasingly global and digital world"	Standards in six areas: Creativity and Innovation; Communication and Collaboration; Research and Information Fluency; Critical Thinking, Problem Solving, and Decision-Making; Digital Citizenship; Technology Operations and Concepts

When we examined the sets of standards focused on teacher education, we found several common themes, and we were struck by the ways in which these themes align with principles of effective online instruction. In the next section, we discuss prominent themes we found across InTASC, IRA, and CAEP documents related to standards for teacher preparation.

THEMES ACROSS STANDARDS FOR TEACHER PREPARATION

Accountability for Effective Performance

The 2011 InTASC Model Core Teaching Standards highlight "the delineation of knowledge, dispositions, and performances as a way to probe the complexity of the teacher's practice. The relationship among the three have been reframed, however, putting performance first—as the aspect that can be observed and assessed in teaching practice" (Council of Chief State School Officers, 2011, p. 6). Similarly, the 2010 IRA Standards emphasize the collection of evidence that demonstrates competence for each of its standards for reading professionals, with examples that focus on application of knowledge. Recent reports advocate a more seamless alignment between the goals of teacher education and the responsibilities of professional practice in K–12 settings. In other words, those who successfully complete our programs of study should also be successful in their future work with K–12 students, such that their accountability in this regard becomes our accountability (American Association of Colleges for Teacher Education [AACTE], 2011).

One of the unique features of our work as literacy teacher educators is that it is heavily focused on practice. The 2010 NCATE report *Transforming Teacher Education Through Clinical Practice* suggests that clinical experience must be an integral and dynamic component of teacher education (National Council for Accreditation of Teacher Education [NCATE], 2010). This is especially true in literacy education, with its long tradition of reflective practice coupled with practical experiences in reading clinics, professional development schools, and other practice sites.

Technology Integration

The NCATE report Transforming Teacher Education Through Clinical Practice also highlights the importance of technology in high-impact teacher preparation, suggesting that new technologies can "promote enhanced productivity, greater efficiencies, and collaboration through learning communities" (2010, p. 6). This is also a key theme in the standards to which K–12 students are held, as illustrated in the Standards for the English Language Arts, jointly determined by IRA and NCTE (1996) nearly 2 decades ago, and the more recent Common Core State Standards (National Governors Association Center for Best Practices & Council of Chief State School Officers, 2010), which have been adopted by nearly all states. In other words, teachers are expected to regularly and wisely use technology tools to support teaching and learning, and their role as literacy teachers demands that their students be equally equipped to use technology tools to locate, synthesize, and communicate information. In this regard, the Common Core State Standards reiterate, and tie to learning outcomes, what has been articulated both by the International Society for Technology in Education Standards for Students (2012) and by the IRA in its Position Statement on New Literacies and 21st Century Technologies (2009).

Inquiry Learning

Problem based learning (PBL) is highlighted in the NCATE report, serving an array of purposes, including developing and interpreting assessments, problem-solving around collaboration, and professional decisionmaking. At the heart of PBL, according to An and Reigeluth (2008), is "an authentic, complex, and ill-structured problem" that students work to solve collaboratively (p. 1). PBL and other inquiry-based approaches to instruction emphasize careful examination of multiple dimensions of a problem or a case and the well-reasoned application of domain-specific knowledge. Research supports PBL as a way to engage learners, promote in-depth understanding and higher-order thinking, and foster self-directed learning. In applied fields, such as medicine and education, PBL allows students to practice the types of thinking and decisionmaking required in the field. In online learning environments, PBL encourages the active, social construction of knowledge and works against what could become static, one-dimensional learning.

Collaboration in Interactive Professional Communities

Increasingly, standards documents focus not only on what teachers need to know and be able to do with their students, but also on what they need to know and be able to do as members of communities of professional practice. Professional development is no longer viewed as the occasional workshop delivered to teachers, but instead as an ongoing process, as teachers regularly assume the role of both learner and teacher among colleagues. Professional Learning Communities (PLCs) are common in schools, and they reflect the move away from viewing teaching as an individual act, and toward the understanding that teaching is done best with the support of collaborative teams.

In all, there is a move toward transformation in teaching. In fact, according to the Council of Chief State School Officers (2011), the Model Core Teaching Standards

> articulate what effective teaching and learning look like in a transformed public education system—one that empowers every learner to take owner-ship of their learning, that emphasizes the learning of content and application of knowledge and skill to real world problems, that values the differences each learner brings to the learning experience, and that leverages rapidly changing learning environments by recognizing the possibilities they bring to maximize learning and engage learners. (p. 3)

We find it striking that some of the major themes appearing across standards are also central considerations in online teaching and learning. These themes, as well as the broader theme of transformation, have permeated earlier chapters of this book. Major changes—such as moving from a face-to-face to an online learning environment—invite but certainly do not ensure transformation. In this book, we have focused on the invitation to transform your practice by shifting your perspective and appropriating new tools for teaching and learning. At this point, we will consider more directly the intersection of online teaching with the key domains of literacy practice that drive our teacher education.

CONSIDERING KEY DOMAINS OF LITERACY PRACTICE

The chapters on building and sustaining learning communities and tools for constructive learning suggest many online instructional practices that also support the dispositions we are trying to engender among our students: an inquiry stance toward problem solving, the ability to work collaboratively and be co-learners with colleagues and students alike, and an understanding that professional development is a lifelong process. In Chapter 3, we presented a variety of tools and ways they could be used to support constructive learning along Bloom's digital technology hierarchy (Churches, 2009). We now want to extend this conversation by considering more specifically the domains of focus in literacy teacher education. Within these domains we want to remember that we are concerned with students' growing knowledge, practical competencies, and dispositions as literacy professionals. In selecting our domains of focus, we drew heavily on the IRA Standards for Reading Professionals (IRA, 2010). Understanding that there are any number of ways to approach teaching and learning within these domains, and that these domains are not mutually exclusive, our examples are not meant to be prescriptive but instead to suggest possible ways to think about blending our specific instructional goals as literacy teacher educators with a selection of technology tools and learning activities. Within these examples, you will see careful consideration of formative and summative assessment; opportunities to scaffold learning; and the use of several technology tools that can be used not only by our students as a means of fulfilling course requirements, but can also be used by our students in their K–12 classrooms, as a means of expanding the literacy opportunities they provide their students.

Here, we address six domains that we have termed as follows:

- Core Knowledge
- Comprehensive Curriculum and Evidence-Based Instruction
- Assessment, Evaluation, and Data-Driven Decisionmaking
- Diversity and Social Justice
- Co-construction of a Dynamic, Interactive Literate Environment
- Lifelong Learning and Professional Leadership

Core Knowledge

We use the term *core knowledge* much like IRA uses the term *foundational knowledge*, namely, to refer to the major theoretical understandings, seminal research, and best practices that are central to our field. As defined by IRA, this standard includes student understanding of

> major theories and empirical research that describe the cognitive, linguistic, motivational, and sociocultural foundations of reading and writing development, processes, and components, including word recognition, language comprehension, strategic knowledge, and reading–writing connections. . . . the historically shared knowledge of the profession and changes over time in the perceptions of reading and writing development, processes, and components. (IRA, 2010, p. 18)

This body of knowledge is important to our students' abilities to analyze and understand factors associated with demonstrations of reading and writing among a wide variety of learners, to interrogate their own practice, and to read published theoretical pieces with understanding and a critical analysis. Susan teaches a course in which students engage with major theoretical perspectives in the field by reading the work of James Gee, Ken Goodman, John Guthrie, Donald Leu, Louis Moll, Ernest Morrell, Louise Rosenblatt, Roger Shuy, Keith Stanovich, David

LaBerge and Jay Samuels, Lev Vygostky, and others through primary source documents and major research reviews and syntheses. The overarching goal of this class is that students understand, articulate, critique, and apply major theories and research findings in the field of literacy. With this learning outcome in mind, Susan devotes much time to explaining new constructs and defining key vocabulary that might be unknown to students in the class, supporting their growing frameworks for understanding, providing opportunities to link theory to practice, and providing forums for demonstrating and cumulatively building knowledge.

One way Susan highlights core knowledge is to use discussion boards both for building community and building knowledge. Susan has found it helpful to establish a large group discussion board forum that is focused on new terms and concepts that students have encountered in the readings. She encourages students to post questions about new vocabulary they have seen in the readings. She uses this space for students to hash out definitions with the rest of the class when a particular word or concept remains unclear.

In addition to the use just described, the discussion board serves a variety of purposes related to the primary learning goals for the class, and also serves to maintain a learning community in which understandings are socially constructed. Small-group discussion board conversations are guided by prompts that are designed to move students from receptive to expressive understanding of key concepts and to encourage connections between theory and personal practice/professional experience (which can be thought of as a form of *text-to-self connections*) as well as connections among a variety of theories (a form of *text-to-text connections*) and connections between theory and observations of practice in the field or current policy initiatives (a form of *text-to-world connections*). Whenever possible, parallels are drawn between what teachers are doing as students in our graduate classes and what their students can do in their K–12 classes. Students' responses to the prompts, and their responses to one another's prompts, provide a window into their current understandings, which serves as a source for formative assessment and allows the instructor to correct misunderstandings and scaffold expanded understandings. The rubric used to evaluate discussion board participation, found in Appendix B, is meant to reflect the thinking and communication processes that Susan hopes students will employ.

At the end of the class, students submit their *Theoretical Perspectives Project* (see Appendix A), which serves as data for summative assessment of what they've learned. In the Spotlight section of this chapter, Susan describes the challenges of bringing this project to an online setting for the first time.

Comprehensive Curriculum and Evidence-Based Instruction

Research on best practices in literacy instruction continually illustrates the importance of balanced, integrated, comprehensive, evidence-based approaches to student achievement (Allington & Johnston, 2002; Gambrell, Malloy, & Mazzoni, 2011; Pressley, Wharton-McDonald, Hampson, & Echevarria, 1998). The IRA standard focused on Curriculum and Instruction identifies the following key elements:

> Candidates use foundational knowledge to design or implement an integrated, comprehensive, and balanced curriculum . . . use appropriate and varied instructional approaches, including those that develop word recognition, language comprehension, strategic knowledge, and reading–writing connections . . . [and] use a wide range of texts (e.g., narrative, expository, and poetry) from traditional print, digital, and online resources. (IRA, 2010, p. 20)

In Chapter 4, Lane described an assignment in which students are required to design a lesson based on the ReadWriteThink (www.readwritethink.org) lesson plan template, incorporating their knowledge of theory and research, incorporating technology, and engaging in peer feedback as part of the lesson design process. Here, we will look at lesson planning and instruction within the context of clinical experience, with an emphasis on providing timely, accessible feedback.

Many graduate programs have a clinical component that includes assessment, evaluation, and tailored instruction with one or more students who are experiencing difficulty with reading. In Susan's online program, students engage in a year-long clinical experience in which they work with a series of students across the K–12 spectrum. Throughout this experience, students plan and implement instruction through thematic, integrated lessons addressing word recognition, vocabulary and comprehension, and writing. Ongoing data collection and reflection accompany each set of weekly lessons, and these plans and reflections are submitted to the instructor for feedback and evaluation. Students use the same lesson plan format across the entire year and are expected to demonstrate increasing levels of competency over time. While there is a detailed rubric designed both to guide students in their lesson planning process and to guide instructors in lesson plan evaluation, students have communicated that rubric completion and written comments are not always adequate supports for improving their lesson planning processes and documentation of planning. Further, expediency in providing feedback is critical because students use instructor feedback as they design their next set of lessons.

One of the challenges that many online learners face is the proliferation of words on a screen. We have previously highlighted the importance of using more than one medium for communicating with students, especially as this relates to the relational aspect of teaching and ways to sustain communities of learners. However, it is also important to avoid overreliance on written text as the sole means of providing feedback on student work. In our classes, we have found that students often struggle to understand written feedback, even when it is connected to (what we hope are) well-structured assessment rubrics. Therefore, we have found it helpful to use tools such as Knovio, Screencast-o-matic, VoiceThread, and Podcasts to share short (3–5-minute) audio or video clips focused on specific aspects of student work. These can be shared with students individually, with small groups, or with the entire class, depending upon who needs what sort of feedback.

Another way to support students online is to incorporate instructional videos for student self-assessment and competency demonstration. Shared teaching videos can be a powerful catalyst for teacher professional growth (Peterson, 2013). In Susan's Reading Endorsement program, students regularly share video of themselves with their instructors and assigned mentors, in order to receive feedback on how they teach, assess, and interact with students. Before sharing the videos, they complete a self-assessment sheet, which is focused on specific dimensions of teaching and assessment articulated in the IRA Standards for Reading Professionals. They then edit the videos down to 15-minute clips to share with instructors.

One way to extend this learning opportunity is to incorporate video sharing and/or peer assessment into the process. Video sharing allows students to learn by watching others and also stimulates reflection on their own practices. Peer assessment allows students to step into a coaching role, attending not only to what they observe and do not observe in their peers' videos, but also to how they will share that information in a constructive, collegial manner. Students often see dimensions of teaching, learning, and assessment in others' interactions with students that they do not see in their own. Peer assessment, then, increases the capacity for everyone's learning. Providing direction to students regarding safe, private ways to upload their videos can be a challenge. It is worthwhile to confer with technical support personnel in your university or school setting, to consider options that work best within your context and within your course management system.

Assessment, Evaluation, and Data-Driven Decisionmaking

Increasingly, schools are calling on teachers to be proficient in ongoing data collection, the interpretation of data, the explanation of data to multiple stakeholders, and the use of data for instructional decisionmaking. Aligned with this is the ability to use a variety of assessment tools and techniques and to make wise decisions about which tools and techniques to use for which purposes. Expectations for assessment and evaluation reflected in the IRA Standards for Reading Professionals include the ability to

> understand types of assessments and their purposes, strengths, and limitations . . . select, develop, administer, and interpret assessments, both traditional print and electronic, for specific purposes . . . use assessment information to plan and evaluate instruction . . . [and] communicate assessment results and implications to a variety of audiences. (2010, pp. 22, 24)

Video clips of diagnostic sessions with students allow instructors to provide specific feedback on the way in which tools and techniques are being implemented and support the instructor in understanding whether resulting data are being interpreted accurately and/or reasonably. Other ways to support and gauge learning include structured observation of varied assessment tools and techniques and evaluation of work samples in the community.

A quick search of YouTube or TeacherTube will turn up numerous examples of teachers assessing literacy behaviors, using a variety of tools. These examples can be fruitful for helping students learn how best to administer an assessment or to help students to determine the strengths and limitations of specific approaches. Of course, there are also opportunities to critique assessment practices, including the degree to which particular assessments have been administered correctly and the types of information gleaned from particular assessments.

In addition to watching other videos, there are a number of ways that students in online literacy education courses can work together to evaluate student work. Students can be assigned to view work samples that have been posted online or can upload samples of their own students' work (without identifying information and with guardian permission, of course) for this purpose. Many state departments of education have samples of student work associated with assessments, and other websites, such as the Reading and Writing Project operated by Teachers College, include student work samples. Websites such as Dropbox support the sharing of documents among students in the class. Using Dropbox would allow students to share their own examples of student work as well as observations and questions about the work that has been shared.

Diversity and Social Justice

As literacy teacher educators, we aim to provide our students with the knowledge, resources, dispositions, and strategies for assessment and instruction that maximize learning for all students, regardless of race, ethnicity, class, gender, religion, language, or sexual orientation. This requires us to engage in instruction that challenges stereotypes and deficit thinking. The IRA standard that is focused on diversity includes the following key elements:

> Candidates recognize, understand, and value the forms of diversity that exist in society and their importance in learning to read and write . . . use a literacy curriculum and engage in instructional practices that positively impact students' knowledge, beliefs, and engagement with the features of diversity, [and] develop and implement strategies to advocate for equity. (2010, pp. 24, 26)

As mentioned previously in this book, online teaching often results in an increase in diversity among students in any given class, and we have found this characteristic to be particularly beneficial in working toward these goals. Still, as the teaching force remains fairly homogeneous with respect to gender, race, and native language, addressing issues of diversity occurs best when time has been taken to create strong learning communities, as suggested in Chapter 2.

One assignment that has been used often in teacher education programs is a version of the *literacy autobiography*, in which students reflect upon their experiences with reading and writing over the course of their lives. This assignment invites students to think about the role of literacy in their lives and the lives of those significant members of their lives, as well as some of the factors that have shaped their relationship with literacy and their sense of self as a literate being. The *multi-genre literacy autobiography* widens the lens through which students can investigate and present their literacy life stories. They are no longer bound to words or to the genre of "the college paper." Students can use words, images, song, sound effects, and more to represent the role(s) of literacy in their lives. Further, they are invited to mix together genres such as a line of poetry, a phrase in a magazine article, a newspaper headline, and song lyrics, in order to capture variation and texture that may characterize their experiences and perspectives. In addition to raising students' awareness of their own reading and writing habits and dispositions, one dimension of the IRA standards, this activity can also be used early in class to help students get to know one another. If you choose to use students' autobiographies for this purpose, we suggest inviting students to share an excerpt of their autobiography with their peers, rather than the entire exhibit. It is important to be aware that for many students, this assignment is fraught with risk, as who they are or have been, as literate beings, and their experiences with literacy over the span of their lives may not fit their perception of a "good literacy teacher." One of the reasons this assignment is so powerful is that it draws students' attention to the fact that who they are, as literate beings, is complex, multidimensional, and tied to their life histories. When students share portions of their autobiographies with one another, they become aware of the diverse ways in which even a group of teachers are literate and have experienced literacy in their lives. The act of getting to know others in this way can begin to shift stereotypes that students may have held prior to this point.

Another assignment that can be done is a *multi-genre literacy biography*. This assignment is similar to the one described above, but instead of focusing on self, it requires students to focus outside of self. Specifically, students are required to get to know a K–12 student, preferably one they don't already know very well, and one who is different from them based on types of diversity identified by Tatum (2011) in his review of diversity and literacy (e.g., gender, native language, religion, race, ethnicity, sexual orientation). The goal of this assignment is for students to gain an understanding of the many ways in which literacy manifests itself, some of which may look like "school literacy" and much of which may not. By interviewing and observing the selected student (after obtaining student and guardian permission), students then construct a literacy biography of this student, paying particular attention to demonstrations of his or her funds of knowledge (Moll, Amanti, Neff, & Gonzalez, 1992). A funds-of-knowledge perspective focuses on the knowledge, competencies, and types of literacies that students have gained from participation in their cultural and linguistic communities of practice and assumes that these are resources that can be utilized in school. Unlike deficit perspectives, the focus is not on what students don't know or haven't experienced, but instead on what they do know, have experienced, and can leverage as resources for learning in school. With careful guidance, this assignment has the potential to challenge stereotypical thinking about students viewed as "other." The decision to design this learning experience as a multigenre project stimulates students in locating multiple literacies in the life of their selected students. Instead of simply talking about multiple literacies, the format of the project parallels its content; the project itself is an expression of multiple literacies, *requiring* the student to go beyond traditional notions of literacy.

Co-construction of a Dynamic, Interactive Literate Environment

Across sets of standards for teacher education, attention is paid to the environment within which teaching occurs—the physical, cognitive, and affective spaces that teachers create, in community with their students, to foster learning. For literacy teachers, it is important for this environment to support achievement for all students. Therefore, the co-construction of a literate environment across the spectrum of literacies required in the 21st century, including print, digital, and online, is vital. The IRA standards (2010) emphasize the ability to design

> the physical environment to optimize students' use of traditional print, digital, and online resources in reading and writing instruction . . . [and] a social environment that is low risk and includes choice, motivation, and scaffolded support to optimize students' opportunities for learning to read and write. (p. 28)

Further, IRA highlights the use of

> routines to support reading and writing instruction (e.g., time allocation, transitions from one activity to another, discussions, and peer feedback) . . . [and] a variety of classroom configurations (i.e., whole class, small group, and individual) to differentiate instruction. (p. 28)

It is important to note the ways in which our online environments serve as a model of an interactive, dynamic, co-constructed setting for learning. Much of what we have discussed in earlier chapters speaks to this modeling function, and here we wish to point out the importance of being explicit with students about what makes the online learning environment a co-constructed literate environment. One way to do this is to check in with students by incorporating reflection in this area into discussion boards or VoiceThread posts. Students can contemplate and respond to questions such as: What do you notice about how you're interacting with our online learning environment? What are you doing here that you could also do with your own students? In addition, it is important to provide learning opportunities that focus students' attention on robust K–12 literacy environments.

Another way of supporting this goal would be to create a *literacy environment observation and feedback* assignment. Video clips showing literacy environments allow students to view a wide variety of classrooms, across grade levels, noting what they observe, what they might appropriate, and what they modify for use with their students. They might view video or photos of one another's classrooms, or classrooms in their schools (with permission of the classroom teacher, of course), and/or videos posted by teachers around the world. The Annenberg Foundation's Annenberg Learner site (www.learner.org) has a wealth of rich videos in which teachers exhibit and discuss exemplary practice within their classroom spaces. Here the literacy environments, along with teachers' reflections on them, might serve as a catalyst for discussion and planning. By viewing various literacy environments that have been created by real teachers in real schools, students gain an understanding of "what it looks like" to enact a comprehensive literacy environment. Figure 5.2 shows a checklist that students can use to begin to think about elements of a co-constructed literate environment as they appear in video clips or in their own classrooms. It is closely aligned with IRA's Literate Environment standard.

Finally, one can create a multimedia presentation for students and families. One of the challenges of creating powerful literacy environments is recognizing the balance between fostering the environment and establishing the conditions under which the environment can be co-created with students in K–12 settings. One way to address this, while simultaneously supporting students in the integration of technology into their teaching, is to have students design a literacy experience in which their students design a multimedia presentation of the classroom literacy

Figure 5.2. Quick Checklist of Items Associated with a Co-constructed Literate Environment

Item	☑	Notes (Observations, Questions, Reflections)
Physical environment includes traditional print, digital, and online resources, all of which are easily accessible to students.		
Students are observed using a variety of resources (e.g., traditional print, digital, and online) for reading and writing.		
There is a variety of grouping configurations such as one-on-one, small group, and whole group to differentiate instruction.		
There is evidence of a supportive social environment that is low risk, includes choice, and is motivating students.		
A variety of scaffolds are used to maximize learning.		
Routines are used effectively to support reading and writing instruction.		
English language learners are encouraged and given many opportunities to use English.		
Multiple literacies are reflected in, and incorporated into, the environment in order to maximize learning.		
The environment has been co-constructed by the teacher and students and is consistently adapted to meet the changing needs of the class.		

environment (e.g., KidPix Slideshow; Prezi). Presentations such as these typically illustrate the integration of literacy throughout the school day, and across disciplines and genres, in keeping with the goals of the Common Core State Standards (National Governors Association Center for Best Practices & Council of Chief State School Officers, 2010). When K–12 students create the representation of their classrooms, from the perspective of literacy learning, they interact with and "own" the environment in important ways.

Lifelong Learning and Professional Leadership

Increasingly, our field has recognized the importance of ongoing, context-specific professional development (Peterson, 2013), and the need for those with in-depth knowledge and experience to take leadership roles in their schools, districts, and states. In recent years, the International Reading Association has sounded a call for literacy leaders who can work collaboratively to support and empower teachers and who can effectively communicate with a variety of stakeholders as advocates of best-practice approaches to reading instruction. Specifically, the organization calls for literacy teachers who possess

> foundational knowledge of adult learning theories and related research about organizational change, professional development, and school culture . . . positive dispositions related to their own reading and writing and the teaching of reading and writing, and [who] pursue the development of individual professional knowledge and behaviors. (IRA, 2010, p. 30)

These teachers should also possess:

> as well as the ability to participate in, design, facilitate, lead, and evaluate effective and differentiated professional development programs . . . [and] understand and influence local, state, or national policy decisions. (IRA, 2010, p. 32)

The Professional Development Experience, developed by Drs. Kathy Hoover, Chet Laine, and Susan Watts Taffe (see Appendix A: Assignment 5), is used to assess the candidate's ability to plan effective teacher professional development to meet the literacy needs of students across the grades. It is designed to provide students with the knowledge, skills, and resources needed to take a leadership role in designing effective instruction, developing and evaluating curriculum materials, creating a literate environment, and facilitating teacher professional development.

SPOTLIGHT: SUSAN'S REFLECTIONS ON THE
THEORETICAL PERSPECTIVES PROJECT

The purpose of the Theoretical Perspectives Project is for students to demonstrate understanding of major theories in the field and to articulate a personal professional perspective, reflective of their critical analysis of the major theories as well as consideration of their own experiences in the field. When I was new to online teaching, I held the disposition that I think many others in this position do: Instead of thinking about how this project could be different online, I was focused on how to reproduce the face-to-face version in the new online format. I thought about how students could create a poster or a model, then photograph it and upload the photo for sharing. I knew there were tools the students could use to share audio that could accompany these photos, but I did not feel confident that I could ask students to incorporate these tools when I was just learning how to use them myself. In the end, the move online took all of my time and energy, and so I dropped the dynamic, interactive portion of this project. Students submitted a paper only, with the invitation to include a diagram or concept map within the paper.

The original project was aligned with the 2003 IRA Standards for Reading Professionals. When the revised standards were published in 2010, I wanted to adjust the assignment accordingly. In particular, I wanted the project to serve as a demonstration of students' specific understandings of theories that might be categorized as cognitive, linguistic, sociocultural, and motivational (referenced in IRA Standard 1.1) as well as their understanding of the role of diversity in literacy learning (referenced in IRA Standard 4.1). As I thought about how to accomplish this, I realized that I needed an assignment with more robust guidelines and I needed to scaffold student work on this project over many weeks of the term.

The original version of this project included directions to students to begin several weeks before the due date and to bring questions to class as they arose. Students accomplished this. While this approach allowed for instructor support and scaffolding along the way, it did not ensure it. As I worked to re-create this project, my goal was to embed formative assessment and scaffolding within the assignment design. This led to a series of shorter papers that built on one another toward the final project. Due dates for these subassignments were staggered, beginning about one-third of the way into the term. Formative assessment occurred, as students were given feedback but were not graded on each paper leading up to the final project. Additionally, reading their shorter papers as the term unfolded allowed me to adjust my instruction based on how they were approaching their work.

Over time, as I talked with colleagues about what they were doing in their online classes, and I became familiar with more technology
tools myself, I began to recognize the limitations of trying to reproduce
the face-to-face interactive sessions online. I decided that in addition
to sharing ideas with peers, the critical dimension of those sessions was
that students represented their knowledge with a model of some sort—a
physical structure or visual representation. Technology tools can be used
to videotape or photograph such models, which might be constructed
with any type of medium, usually one with which the student is very
comfortable and, thus, provides an easy way for him or her to think
about abstract theoretical constructs in a more concrete way (e.g., using
the metaphor of cooking to represent the reading process or building
an electric circuit to show what happens when someone reads). But
technology tools offer additional options, such as video (e.g., iMovie or
YouTube), captioned or narrated slide shows (e.g., Prezi or Ignite Presentations), or photos coupled with simple text, and dynamic concept
maps (e.g., Popplit). This portion of the change process brought me full
circle when I realized that if I wanted my students to represent knowledge in multiple ways, preferably appropriating at least a few technology tools to do so, then I needed to model this. This realization led me to
go through the course and find ways to represent knowledge beyond a
narrated PowerPoint.

TENSIONS, RENEGOTIATIONS, AND CRITICAL REFLECTIONS

In this chapter, we have shared some of the processes and products that
reflect our ongoing journey to meet several student learning objectives
that are associated with literacy teacher education programs. The work
we've shared is not done, but is, as always, in progress. For many of us,
this fact alone is a critical tension—the reality that online course design
and instruction is never finished "once and for all," but instead consistently developing, advancing swiftly at times and slowly at other times.
Of course, high-quality instruction is never static, a fact that is true both
in face-to-face and online learning environments. However, the rate at
which technology tools change and new tools emerge does lend a unique
quality of change to the work we do. With the myriad responsibilities
assumed by most faculty (e.g., research and writing, administration, and
professional service), it is important to develop a strategy and structure
for improving course design that allows for growth and productivity in
the other areas of our professional lives.

In addition to the ever-present dilemma of time constraints, we are
challenged to operate in a space riddled with unknowns, especially at the

beginning. Take, for example, a new assignment that requires students to use technology, and its accompanying rubric. We have found that it is almost always necessary to revise rubrics based on the first round of use, as it is only when students do the assignment that we determine what is possible. New assignments also bring renegotiation. When we invite students to demonstrate their knowledge in multiple and textured ways, we need to renegotiate with ourselves what it is we are actually looking for. Criteria for success are no longer tied to long-established traditions such as the standard written paper. Negotiating this requires a presence that is both time-consuming and energizing.

As we renegotiate with ourselves, we also renegotiate with students, who themselves must step into the unknown and away from what may be a comfortable tradition. Students who are new to online learning often experience frustration and anxiety, as they must expend a great deal of time and energy learning how to learn in entirely new ways. In our experience, students who have a record of success in traditional settings are often the most distressed by the lack of familiarity and resulting underconfidence they may initially experience as online learners. Until they become familiar with the new learning tools they will be using, it is very difficult for them (and often for the instructor) to distinguish between their understanding of the content and their proficiency with the tools used to acquire, interact with, and demonstrate understanding of the content. On the other hand, students whose knowledge and competencies were not fully reflected in traditional learning experiences may gravitate to new options and will often take leadership roles in the class that they have not previously assumed. This renegotiation of competence mirrors that which occurs in K–12 settings, when technology is used to increase access to learning for all students. In designing online learning experiences, it is helpful to continually consider this question: How can I support students in being successful both with the content and with the tools needed to engage with and demonstrate knowledge of the content?

Finally, for many teacher educators, there are obvious tensions embedded in the use of standards to guide and assess teaching and learning. However, we believe that standards can provide an anchor in online teaching, where the draw of so many new and interesting tools can sometimes be overwhelming. It is easy to be tempted to do something because we can, rather than because it is tied to what we want our students to learn. A careful consideration of the standards that drive our practice (whether provided by a professional organization or developed within specific programs of study) is important to ensuring that literacy teacher education, done online, works—and works well. We have found that taking on this work in community helps us to maximize our effectiveness. In this regard, we hope this book is a helpful tool.

Activities to Try

- Look through the standards that drive your teaching—pick one that you feel could use some more attention and brainstorm some ways you can reach that standard in your online teaching.
- Pick an activity that you currently use and change it to reflect a PBL (problem-based learning) approach.
- Think through how your students communicate their understanding of the core knowledge needed to teach K–12 literacy.
- Think of a way you could use videos to support reflection and deepen understanding of curriculum and evidenced-based instruction.
- Find and watch some videos of teachers assessing readers or using assessment data. How could you use these in your teaching?
- Think of how you could use the multi-genre literacy autobiography/biography in your teaching.
- Pick a video from the Annenberg Learner site (or another site) and use the checklist to evaluate a literate environment.

VOICES FROM THE FIELD

Literacy teachers are engaged with colleague conversations, teacher-based team meetings, data meetings, and a multitude of job-embedded professional development opportunities on a regular basis. Numerous teachers are trying to find a balance between their life/work, and online learning can allow teachers the freedom to have some flexibility as they attempt to balance their school and personal lives. If the purpose of literacy education is to allow time for teachers to explore many ideas so they can grow in their knowledge and perhaps question and challenge their own belief systems, it is important to empower teachers so they have the choice to explore professional development that best fits their own professional needs.

My first experience teaching online courses was working as an electronic learning facilitator. Individual school buildings selected "best practice" courses for the staff and there were face-to- face sessions in addition to online discussion boards and assignments. The teachers already taught together, so they had a sense of community that was enhanced as they shared their own experiences and struggles and interacted with and discussed mentor texts. In addition, the teachers had assignments that allowed them to practice strategies with their students and to collect data that were shared with their colleagues. Teachers talked about literacy issues, and their shared experiences led to a heightened sense of intimacy within the online discussion boards. A sense of trust and shared vulnerability was embraced. These were some of my best online teaching experiences, not because they were required by the school/building or state but because the shared accountability propelled the teachers to work together as they achieved common goals.

The future of online literacy instruction is promising if there is time and space built into the course for a multitude of student engagement that will allow them to build a sense of community within the virtual classroom environment. My best experience as an electronic instructor blended both the virtual and face-to-face worlds and allowed for both formal and informal interaction among the participants. Online literacy learning will continue to thrive, but a multitude of active engagement must be provided.

—Eileen Diamond, transformation specialist,
Ohio Department of Education, Office of School Turnaround

CHAPTER 6

Changing the Landscape for Reading Professionals Through Online Learning

Questions to Ponder

- What are the advantages of blended, or hybrid, course models?
- How can online and blended learning support job-embedded teacher professional development?
- As a learner yourself, what are the most powerful professional development experiences you've been a part of?
- As a leader or facilitator, what are the most powerful professional development experiences you've been a part of?
- What are the similarities and differences between working with teachers within the context of a university course and working with teachers within the context of a professional development effort?

In a recent presentation at the conference of the Literacy Research Association Kevin Leander (2012) said, "There is no cyberspace." Observing that we send text messages while sitting on a park bench, play a board game with our kids while simultaneously checking Facebook, talk with students by email and by Skype, he asserted that cyberspace is not "out there," but rather all around us. There are no longer clear boundaries between virtual and physical spaces, but instead a single space, including both the physical and the virtual. This idea is pertinent to the two topics we will explore in this chapter.

Although this book's primary focus has been on teaching and learning within the context of university coursework, we believe the key points we've discussed are applicable to teacher learning and professional growth in a variety of settings. Our first discussion focuses on dimensions of online learning as they apply to choosing the best platform for creating learning experiences. While we believe that much of what has been discussed in previous chapters relates to different formats for online learning, we also recognize that there are several decisions that need to be made when thinking about how to present online learning experiences. The second part of this chapter will specifically address professional development. In fact, research on effective teacher professional development highlights many of the same features that characterize robust online teaching and learning. These include attention to the role of the professional development facilitator (with implications for her or his identity construction), the importance of learning communities that are sustained over time, active teacher engagement, and the social construction of learning.

BLENDED LEARNING ENVIRONMENTS

Complexity of Synchrony and Time in Blended Learning

Stacey and Gerbic (2008) asserted that there was little research on effective teaching and learning in blended environments, contending that, compared to both face-to-face and online instruction, "For students and teachers, there is a higher degree of complexity in dealing with two environments; there are also issues of legitimacy and acceptance when online environments are integrated with traditional face-to-face settings" (p. 964). One of the reasons for this complexity (and the reason we prefer the term *blended* over *hybrid*) is that a blended course done well is more than the sum of its parts. More than the combination of two disparate learning environments, it is "the thoughtful fusion of face-to-face and online learning experiences" (Garrison & Vaughn, 2008). Further, the pedagogical considerations of each of these environments informs the other, such that the all-around experiences of teaching and learning are transformed.

On the surface, blended learning might be considered the best of both worlds. In order to maximize the integration of these worlds, however, it is important to consider two key constructs: synchrony and time. The first consideration is the balance of synchronous activity and asynchronous activity. Often, face-to-face learning is thought of as synchronous whereas online learning is considered asynchronous. While it is true that online learning can be highly asynchronous, today's tools allow for many forms of synchrony, as discussed previously in this book. And certainly we have all taught "live" classes that were less engaging to our students than we had hoped, which illustrates that teaching can be synchronous without the intended corollary of synchronous learning. To begin, it is helpful to think about what we see as the benefits of meeting with our students in real time and how we might achieve similar benefits through asynchronous activity. There are many ways to harness the positive elements of real-time interaction in an environment where students and instructor are not all meeting at the same time. See Figure 6.1 for a description of how to capitalize on moving synchronous learning activities to asynchronous opportunities.

Figure 6.1. Enhancing Synchronous Activities with Asynchronous Opportunities

Face-to-Face Activity	Asynchronous Adaptation	Benefits of Shift of Practice
Class Presentations	Have students put PowerPoints, videos, or other presentations online	• Saves time in class from watching each student present • Allows students to view a presentation at different times (not one after another after another) • Viewer can start and stop presentation at any point when it is convenient or if he or she wants to watch something again or slow down a presentation • All students have access to all presentations
Small-Group Discussions	Have students discuss in online discussion groups before class	• Everyone in the group has an equal opportunity to participate • In class each group can share a summary of small group's discussion in order to engage in more whole-group discussion or deeper processing of a concept • All small-group discussions can be viewed by instructor
Video Clips	Put videos online to be watched by students	• Saves class time by not watching videos during class • Ask students to watch a video multiple times for different things (e.g., in the first viewing look for what the teacher does; during the second viewing just watch the students . . .) • Students have the ability to start and stop videos on their own • Play back video parts that are important
Presentation of Content	Have students choose different topics or levels in online presentation of materials	• A great way to differentiate material • Students can have choices of materials based on student interest, need, or level of learning (e.g., if you are new to RTI read this, if you have lots of experience with RTI read this) • Increase motivation and engagement

The second key consideration is the distribution of time. Our discussions in Chapter 4 of the importance both of preplanning for online instruction and checking in regularly throughout the life of the course have serious implications for the ways in which teachers manage their time. The same is true for students in online courses, where most report spending more time than they do in face-to-face courses. But in addition to how much time is spent and how it is spent, it is important to consider the way in which time is distributed online. Specifically, there is the potential for a more even distribution of time across a week that can serve as a support for in-depth knowledge acquisition and long-term learning. When deciding when to balance synchronous with asynchronous experiences, instructors may want to consider which topics would benefit from the increase in time—perhaps more complex topics may be better served in an online component where a student has more time to process and discuss. Synchrony, asynchrony, and diversity in the distribution of time are affordances of blended learning to consider when planning and carrying out instruction.

Characteristics of Effective Blended Learning Environments

In a study of instructors in blended courses, Kaleta, Skibba, and Joosten (2007) found that the initial inclination was to use the face-to-face component of a blended class for interactive activities such as demonstrations and small-group discussions, and to use the online component for independent work, such as reading, written assignments, and individual reflection. However, more experienced blended course instructors created opportunities for reflection, critical analysis, and interaction both online *and* face-to-face. They also cross-referenced experiences across these domains (e.g., referencing themes in students' discussion board posts during face-to-face class meetings or using the online space to extend a learning activity that was started face-to-face), which increased course cohesion and enhanced student learning. More experienced instructors also tended to recognize that a blended course can maximize accessibility by increasing the degree to which different learning styles can be met. They found variation in students' demonstrated learning across the wider variety of platforms available in a blended course.

The authors of this study warned against "course and a half syndrome," which is characterized by teaching a face-to-face class as it has always been taught and simply adding online components to it—in effect, teaching more than one class. This can be tricky terrain when taking a course that was formerly face-to-face and moving it to a blended format. It can be challenging to establish your teacher identity in a blended course as something other than two separate identities: your face-to-face identity, along with its pedagogical style and instructional practices, and your online identity, with its separate pedagogical style and instructional practices. A set of global questions, such as the following, can guide instructional decisionmaking surrounding the face-to-face and online elements, as well as the intentional, focused interplay between the two. We suggest revisiting them briefly each week throughout the course.

- What are your learning objectives for the course?
- How do you want students to interact with the course content?
- What kind of thinking do you want to promote?
- How do you want students to interact with one another as they engage with the course content—both online and face-to-face?

Many of the principles and tools we've discussed in earlier chapters of this book are applicable to blended instruction. Establishing our identities, building and sustaining effective learning communities, and using technology tools that promote active, constructive, and social learning are just as important in blended courses as they are in online courses. Further, blended course instruction tends to require a heightened sense of course management and greater attention to technology than does online instruction. From a management perspective, instructors need to organize and oversee the logistics for face-to-face experiences, online experiences, and the interplay between the two. Additionally, instructors need to address the technology used in the course at the outset (preferably at the first face-to-face meeting with online tutorials available before and after this meeting). Certainly, we cannot assume that online learners will be adept with the technology required in any given course; however, an instructor is more likely in a blended class to encounter students who have had very little experience with the specific tools they will need to be successful in this learning environment. Planned instruction, patience, and preselected, pretested resources (e.g., university-developed tutorials or personally made screen captures) are important to the success of the course. In Figure 6.2, we provide a list of suggestions for implementing an effective blended learning experience.

When we think about how much of our learning experiences could be online and how much can be blended, we need to weigh all of these factors carefully. Choosing the right format for learning is as important as choosing the objectives for what is learned. When deciding on a fully asynchronous model or a blended model or somewhere in between, you want to keep in mind what makes the most sense for you, your content, and your learner.

TEACHER PROFESSIONAL DEVELOPMENT IN THE 21ST CENTURY

Teacher professional development has been a topic of growing interest in the last few decades. Over time, we have come to recognize that effective professional development must be much more than the occasional one-time presentation conducted by an outside expert. In an analysis of well-designed experimental studies, Darling-Hammond, Wei, Andree,

Figure 6.2. Suggestions for Developing an Effective Blended Learning Experience

Objective	Rationale	Suggested Activities
Structure an orientation to your blended design, including attention to technology	Since there are many ways to implement a blended experience, students need to know specifically what it looks like in your course.	• Address how much time will be spent in face-to-face sessions and how much time will be spent online • Discuss the nature of teaching and learning in each of these spaces • Address communication, especially between face-to-face meetings • Model and provide hands-on practice with the technology required • Discuss the writing-intensive nature of the online component • Address the concept of distributed time • Provide tips for time management
Establish and actively maintain your teacher presence	In some ways, teacher presence is supported by the face-to-face interactions in blended environments. However, it can become lost if you assume that by seeing your students in person periodically, your teacher presence is automatically established.	• Based on ideas presented in Chapter 2, reconsider how you establish your presence in person. • Check how this consciousness affects your practice as you work to establish a cohesive presence across your face-to-face and online platforms. Think about how you can be the same teacher across these spaces, though you may employ techniques unique to each space to support your presence and the learning community.
Build (continuously build) the learning community of your class	It is easy to assume that because your students meet together in the same space periodically, they are a learning community. However, not all learners who are grouped together operate as a learning community.	• Establish mechanisms to support your class as a learning community, both face-to-face and online. • Check that your students display dispositions and practices that support the learning community, and determine specific ways to address dispositions and practices that are not in support of this type of community.
Monitor student engagement and student learning	Blended learning offers myriad ways to engage with course content and demonstrate learning. Both can be maximized with careful attention to the types of engagement and learning that occur across activities and platforms (face-to-face and online).	• Revisit Figure 1.1 and ask yourself the questions related to variety in learning activities, pacing, clarity of expectations, teacher-student interactions, modeling, questioning, and promoting independent thinking. Compare and contrast your answers as you think about your face-to-face instruction and your online instruction. • Consider how students respond to the approaches you've identified above. Reflect on what this tells you about them, as a group and individually, as learners. Based on these reflections, how can you adjust your teaching?

Richardson, and Orphanos (2009) found that professional development that positively effects student achievement is:

1. Intensive, ongoing, and connected to practice
2. Focused on student learning and addressing the teaching of specific curriculum content
3. Aligned with school improvement priorities and goals
4. Characterized by strong, collaborative working relationships among teachers
5. Characterized by teacher investment and ownership

That being said, their multiyear study indicated that while teachers typically participate in some form of professional development each year, access to high-quality teacher professional development varies widely. In-depth learning opportunities, professional collaboration around curriculum planning, and funding to support professional development are in short supply. It is against this backdrop that online professional development has gained momentum. Borko, Whitcomb, and Liston (2009) found that professional development programs are "increasingly turning to contemporary innovative technologies as a way to reach large numbers of individuals at costs lower than those associated with physical presence of professional development facilitators" (p. 30). There are many potential benefits of both online and blended models of professional development. For example:

- *Accessibility.* While it is costly to bring in outside consultants and acknowledged experts to share the latest research and evidence-based practices, it is relatively inexpensive to utilize webinars and researcher videos focused on specific topics. Further, teachers who cannot afford to attend annual conventions can access keynote sessions and workshop materials by way of many convention websites.
- *Broadened Community.* Perhaps the most obvious benefit of online professional development is its accessibility to teachers in remote areas, who can join in community with other teachers to address common concerns. Even for teachers who are closer together, there is the opportunity to connect to larger—namely, national and international—communities of practice.
- *Flexibility.* Scheduling is one of the most prevalent barriers to collaborative professional development. Lack of common planning time prevents teachers from sharing and processing ideas together. The asynchronous nature of much of online learning and communication gets around this barrier by

supporting interaction and collaboration in ways that can accommodate multiple schedules.

- *Contextuality.* One of the criticisms of traditional professional development efforts, such as presentation workshops and conferences, is that they occur outside of the context of teachers' daily work. The isolated nature of an inservice-day presentation or a summer workshop can diminish the likelihood of transfer to teachers' daily instruction. By contrast, online professional development can be structured as an ongoing, "always there" opportunity, allowing teachers to partake *as a part of* their regular, daily practice rather than outside of it.

- *Support.* Finally, information and communication technologies can be used to support teachers in systematic ways by providing them with the knowledge and coaching specific to their needs. For new teachers, this support is critical. Using new technologies, new teachers can work with the most experienced and expert mentors, even if they are located in other schools. Further, groups of new teachers within a district can gather virtually, with the support and direction of a mentor or coach.

In the remainder of this chapter, we discuss examples of online professional development, beginning with its role in national literacy organizations. We then address more localized professional development experienced by teachers within the context of a single school or district. Finally, we present guidelines for successful implementation of online professional development experiences.

National and International Contexts for Online Professional Development

IRA and NCTE are two of several large professional organizations that have begun to leverage new information and communication technologies to reach teachers both nationally and around the world. What started primarily as forums for distributing information (e.g., electronic access to journal articles, links to featured print and electronic information resources) has expanded to include multimedia and interactive communication in the form of researcher and teacher blogs, podcasts on topics such as vocabulary learning and comprehension instruction, webinars (both live and recorded) on topics such as the CCSS and RTI, virtual conferences, teacher study groups, and instructional demonstrations by expert teachers in real classrooms. There are also elements of blended learning. Recently, IRA has used its website to host an ongoing conversation about the CCSS, a conversation that began at the face-to-face annual convention. An expert panel that addressed questions at the convention continues to address questions as they are posed by educators around the country.

In addition to "talking with the experts," teachers can share their expertise with one another. This sort of collaboration and sharing is now recognized as central to the improvement of teacher practice. For example, NCTE hosts the Literacy in Learning Exchange, which allows a space for conversation and idea-sharing. Participants can create their own groups or follow groups that have already been created. At the time of this writing the *Journeys in Digital Literacy* group, facilitated by six educators, has the purpose of "grappling with what it means to be literate in today's world" and meets to discuss this topic in a way that applies to their practice in their own classrooms.

Other groups in this space include a multidistrict group focused on culturally mediated writing instruction, a district-based group focused on family literacy, and a school-based group focused on disciplinary writing in history. These are just a few examples of the opportunities available to educators by way of professional organizations.

Local Contexts for Online Professional Development

It is now quite common for school districts to offer online or blended professional development opportunities. For example, a statewide initiative in Maine called the "Cross Disciplinary Network" brought together content area teachers throughout the state to talk together about CCSS. The group met online, through webinars and a social networking site, as well as face-to-face at various schools throughout the state. In Ohio, online opportunities are provided by Educational Service Centers, serving groups of districts in particular geographic regions. Creating these local spaces is easy with open-access Learning Management Systems (LMS) such as Moodle or Google Groups. But just creating a network does not mean it will be effective. Careful thought about the qualities of effective professional development, as well as what is known about the power of well-structured teacher study groups and Professional Learning Communities (PLCs) to transform teacher practice and improve student learning in schools, can help guide online professional development (PD) opportunities.

Learning from Teacher Study Groups and PLCs

Strong teacher study groups and PLCs (DuFour, DuFour, Eaker, & Many, 2010) are powerful because they are focused on building teacher capacity to improve learning among all students. Both forms of professional development rest on the assumption that school improvement is directly related to teacher improvement. Further, it is assumed that teacher improvement occurs when teachers share and engage in critical conversation about their instructional practices, as connected to the examination of student work, such that clear connections between student learning (or lack thereof) and instruction can be drawn. This stance of "collective inquiry," coupled with an action orientation, are also features of effective teacher study groups. According to Taylor (2011), successful study groups include collaborative meetings, the development of action plans, and data-driven decisionmaking as a driver for instructional change. As we've discussed previously, there are a variety of tools that allow for the sharing of student work online coupled with collaborative analysis. Additionally, video sharing options allow teachers to watch one another in action and share feedback.

Guidelines for Successful Online Professional Development

The following guidelines can be used to plan and monitor online and blended professional development efforts. It is important to note that different types of professional development serve different purposes. Therefore, it is important to establish clear goals for the professional development effort and select from among these guidelines those that are most fitting. For example, if the goal is to inform teachers about a new statewide assessment, it would be reasonable to provide access to a recorded webinar on the topic with an opportunity for questions and discussion shortly afterward. On the other hand, if the goal is for teachers to work collaboratively to determine how to align their instruction with the requirements of the new assessment, an online study group or PLC, conducted over a period of weeks or the entire school year, would be the best choice. These are examples of macro decisions regarding the type of learning structured to meet specific goals. Once these decisions are made, a series of micro decisions are required: How long should the effort last? What is the appropriate balance between information provided from outside sources (e.g., professional practice books, video clips illustrating best practice) and information-sharing among teachers themselves? How will teachers become invested in the effort? How will the strengths and limitations of the effort be gauged, so as to inform future professional development planning? Who will be the leader/coordinator of this group? Some guidelines to maximize the potential of online professional development opportunities are as follows:

- *Entrust leadership to a capable individual with a collaborative mindset.* Especially in study groups and PLCs, it is important to have a designated moderator or facilitator who manages the logistics of the group. If collaborative professional development is new to the teachers involved, it is best for this person to bring knowledge and experience related to facilitating professional development. Over time, teacher participants will grow into this role and it might be rotated among group members. Or teachers involved in a group one year may branch off, each leading a group of new teachers the next year. However, as stated earlier in the book, effective learning depends on a strong teacher. Who this teacher is and how his or her role in online PD looks may vary, but it is essential that there is clear leadership—especially at the beginning of a learning group.

- *Develop a protocol to guide your work together.* A clear, consistent structure is critical to success. This protocol should guide the work done collaboratively (e.g., via the Discussion Board or Adobe Connect meetings) as well as the preparation for that work. Gwinn and Watts-Taffe (2013) have used a professional development grid (see Appendix C) as a way to structure teachers in recording and reflecting on their practice in between group meetings. In a year-long study group focused on vocabulary instruction, teachers completed these grids monthly, then submitted them to the group online prior to meeting face-to-face. Using a grid such as this helps group members to stay focused on the work of their learning community, on a day-to-day basis, as they plan, implement, and reflect on instruction. During face-to-face meetings, they provide a concrete guide for group discussion and encourage future planning based on evidence of what has been tried and how it has impacted student learning.

- *Use time wisely.* Although one of the benefits of online professional development is that teachers can participate in ways that fit their schedules, providing deadlines for particular tasks creates accountability and sustains momentum. Within long-term efforts, breaking things into learning chunks or modules is an effective design. Finally, it is important to consider other demands on teacher time according to the school year and to remember that professional development, online or otherwise, is an integral part of a teacher's work, not an add-on. Therefore, it is important to have institutional structures in place that support the time teachers are required to invest. Also, it is important to be realistic about time. Maintaining a group over too long a period of time can result in enthusiasm fizzling out. Also, starting PD at different points in the year (e.g., the beginning versus the end of the year) may also impact a PD's success.

- *Focus on shared goals that are aligned with school improvement priorities.* Effective professional developments needs to connect to tangible products and meaningful, shared goals. A benefit of professional development grids or discussion board prompts that require teachers to analyze their learning to date is the written record of their growth. Connecting online professional development to official teacher improvement plans, required annually in most districts, is another way to ensure that teachers work toward concrete goals and see their professional progress. Skilled facilitators can support teachers in developing shared goals that are aligned with school- or district-improvement goals. This lessens fragmentation of teacher time and energy.

• *Make connections to the wider conversation.* A unique affordance of online teacher professional development is the ease with which local conversations can be connected to district, state, and national conversations. If instructional teams are struggling to implement RTI effectively, they can gather models from and communicate with professionals who are working through similar dilemmas, in any part of the country. As teachers work to implement state initiatives, they can communicate with state departments on questions and needed clarifications. Additionally, as they become more closely connected to the wider conversations in literacy, they become better positioned to influence those conversations by sharing the expertise they've gleaned in their daily work with students.

TENSIONS, RENEGOTIATIONS, AND CRITICAL REFLECTIONS

The question we most commonly ask is the "what" question—what subjects shall we teach? When the conversation goes a bit deeper, we ask the "how" question—what methods and techniques are required to teach well? Occasionally, when it goes deeper still, we ask the "why" question—for what purpose and to what ends do we teach? But seldom, if ever, do we ask the "who" question— who is the self that teaches? How does the quality of my selfhood form—or deform—the way I related to students, my subject, my colleagues, my world?

—Parker Palmer, *The Courage to Teach*

Blended models of instruction and online models of teacher professional development require a shift in our thinking about what it means to teach and facilitate professional growth. Throughout this book, we have considered dimensions of teaching and learning outside of the traditional space of a bricks-and-mortar classroom. We have discovered that this physical space is often accompanied by a cognitive space—particular ways of thinking about and doing the business of teaching and learning. In this chapter, we have further interrupted these notions in order to consider even more ways of doing things differently than we have before. As Leander (2012) asserts, cyberspace is all around us and necessitates that we think differently about how we use this space in ways that enhance our growth as teachers and learners. Conceptually, this challenge—to consider our teaching identities, teacher presence, and participation in communities of practice across physical and virtual spaces simultaneously—might be considered a *challenge of fluidity*. What are the central tenets of our work that manifest themselves across spaces? And what do these manifestations looks like? In what ways do the rapidly evolving tools of new technologies challenge or reinforce the central tenets that drive our work? What pieces of online versus face-to-face environments produce the most effective learning experiences? Questions such as these can be daunting to those of us who seek the satisfaction of closure and completion. However, the effective teaching practice has always been an iterative process. And just as building teacher capacity is the goal of strong professional development, it is the goal—rather, the requirement—of teaching and learning in the 21st century.

We hope this book has stimulated thinking on the questions of *who, what, why,* and *how* as they relate to our work as online teachers who dedicate our daily practice—online, on the ground, and in hybrid spaces—to teaching those who will teach others about reading, writing, thinking, and being in a world of new and expanding technologies. At this point, we hope you will join us in continued conversation about online teaching and learning for literacy professionals. Please visit www.educatingliteracyteachersonline.com for resources connected with this book and opportunities for ongoing professional development in community with others who are teaching and facilitating teacher professional development online.

Activities to Try

- Brainstorm features of a long-term professional development experience for a group of teachers in a single school. Make a list of which elements taken from this chapter you would integrate into the experience. If you are currently teaching a university course, consider whether any of the elements on your list could be integrated into your course.
- Participate in an interactive learning experience offered by IRA, NCTE, or another professional organization. Consider what these experiences have to offer your students or the teachers for whom you facilitate professional development.
- Create a virtual scavenger hunt or "webquest" to take teachers on a tour of a variety of professional development opportunities available online. Whether you are an online course instructor, a blended course instructor, or a professional development facilitator, think of how this activity could be useful to the teachers with whom you work.
- Think through what parts of your face-to-face class could be enhanced by adding a blended feature to this learning experience.

Sample Assignments

ASSIGNMENT 1: DEBATE

This week you will be engaging in a debate on an issue that is relevant to high-stakes assessment. You will be asked to synthesize information that you read, listen to, and view on a topic. You will then be asked to choose a point of view (this may or not be your personal point of view) and engage in a discussion around this perspective. While this exercise is meant to encourage critical engagement and thinking, I do want to remind you of netiquette and respectful dialogue—especially online (where we don't get to see each other's reactions). Please be especially cognizant of what you say; sometimes what we say online is not as "polite" as what we may say face-to-face.

Task

Videos (watch both)

http://www.democracynow.org/2013/1/29/seattles_teacher_uprising_high_school_faculty

http://www.youtube.com/watch?v=NhoTn2IJLk0

Blogs (pick two)

http://seattleducation2010.wordpress.com/2013/03/02/the-opt-out-update/

http://blogs.edweek.org/edweek/District_Dossier/2013/02/the_seattle_boycott_is_not_abo.html

http://www.newyorker.com/online/blogs/newsdesk/2013/03/seattles-low-stakes-testing-trap.html

http://www.thenation.com/blog/172245/movement-end-high-stakes-testing-steps-seattle

Audio/Newspapers (pick one)

http://www.npr.org/2013/01/17/169620124/seattle-high-schools-teachers-toss-districts-test

http://www.washingtonpost.com/blogs/answer-sheet/wp/2013/01/26/teacher-boycott-of-standardized-test-in-seattle-spreads/

Question/Prompt

In any issue there are always two sides. What are the benefits of high-stakes tests? Why do we need them? Why should we get rid of high-stakes tests? What is the argument of the teachers at Garfield? How would/could this look in your grade level? In your school and district?

Group Process

1. Sunday: Meet in your group and decide on group roles
2. Sunday–Wednesday: Read and go to online resources to prepare your answer.
3. Wednesday–Sunday: Discuss the prompt

Group Roles

If there are more than or less than five people in the group, you may adjust this recommendation.

- Pick two people to argue from one side
- Pick two people to argue from the other side
- Pick a moderator

ASSIGNMENT 2: CASE STUDY

Scenario

Read the following information assessment data on a student.

Background Information

Issah is a 14-year-old boy in 8th grade, age 14.1. Based on teacher recommendations and previous test scores, Issah has been placed in a Tier Two literacy class. Issah was recommended for this Tier Two literacy class because he has struggled in his language arts class and his Scholastic Reading Inventory (SRI) scores have been decreasing since 6th grade. His current literacy teacher reports that his SRI score, which demonstrates a student's ability to comprehend, is far below grade level. However, he does not seem to struggle during class discussions and assessments. She hopes to provide instruction that will strengthen his literacy skills and strategies to allow him to become a proficient reader and writer.

The assessments took place in a separate room during his literacy block. In the beginning, Issah was slightly nervous, but cooperative throughout.

He shared that he does not like to read because he has difficulty understanding what he reads and a difficult time reading "big words." Issah does not read outside of class. He answered all of the questions on the assessments.

Tests Administered

Easy Curriculum Based Measure (CBM) Fluency: University of Oregon, 2007 (8th grade)—*Administered to determine his fluency level because fluency affects comprehension.*

- Benchmark 8-1: 134 CWPM (correct words per minute)
- Benchmark 8-2: 137 CWPM
- Benchmark 8-3: 129 CWPM

San Diego Quick Assessment—*Administered to determine his independent reading level.*

- Independent Reading Level: grade 4
- Instructional Reading Level: grade 5
- Frustration Reading Level: grade 6

SRI—*Administered to determine the student's level of comprehension independently.*

- Lexile: 531
- Grade Level: far below
- Performance Standard: below basic
- Comprehension Assessment (classroom summative)

Accelerated Reader Quiz—*Administered to determine the student's comprehension of a class novel.*

- Scored distinguished for 7 out of the 10 questions
- Scored beginning for 3 out of the 10 questions

Morris McCall Spelling List—*Administered to determine the student's phonemic awareness.*

- Number of words correct: 24/50
- Grade Level Equivalent: 4

Question/Prompt

Based on the data above, what instructional recommendations would you make for this student? Think about whole-class instruction, small-group instruction, one–on-one instruction. Also think about assessment in terms of progress monitoring. With your group, come up with an instructional plan for this student.

Reading

Read the three articles assigned for this week: Risko & Walker-Dalhouse (2010), Dennis (2009), and McKenna & Walpole (2005). Also draw upon readings from other weeks. Draw on web resources provided in other modules of the class.

Group Process

1. Sunday: Meet in your group and decide on roles (Each person needs to have a role, which must be different for each case study; you probably will not get each role, since there are only three case studies).
2. Sunday–Wednesday: Read and go to online resources to prepare your answer.
3. Wednesday–Sunday: Discuss the Case Study Question/Prompt.

Group Roles

Everyone in your group needs to choose a role from the following list. Keep in mind that while these are only the roles that each of you will "officially" have in this discussion, every group member is also responsible for participating in all parts of the discussion according to the class discussion board participation rubric. If there are more than four members, two members will need to have the same role.

- *Facilitator:* Initiates discussion, oversees knowledge, organizes flow of discussion, clarifies and summarizes when necessary, elicits participation
- *Recorder:* takes meeting notes, summarizes contributions
- *Case Manager:* this can be the teacher or one of the teachers. This person provides background information (feel free to make this up), and instructional context
- *Literacy Specialist:* provides resources and expertise (draw on the reading and websites)
- *Other:* feel free to create another role as your group sees fit

ASSIGNMENT 3: ASSESSMENT MINI-INQUIRY PROJECT

Overview

In this assignment you will examine literacy assessment in a context broader than your classroom. You will choose your own question and then create a survey that you will be administering to teachers in your school, district, or community (and that can include us). You will analyze these data and report on what you learned to your classmates. You will be working in groups to get support through this process. This project is broken into three tasks, as described below.

Task One

1. In the Johnston and Costello (2005) article the authors assert some *big ideas* about literacy assessment. For example, *some* of the big ideas that they present are:
   - Literacy assessment defines literacy
   - What gets assessed is what gets taught
   - Literacy assessment effects how we organize literacy instruction
   - The validity of an assessment lies in its consequences
   - The teacher is the primary agent of assessment
   - Teachers need both formative and summative assessments
2. Take *one* of these big ideas and create a *smaller measurable question* (the questions can have more than one part). For example, a question could look like:
   - How is formative assessment used to drive literacy instruction in 4th- and 5th- grade classrooms?
   - What types of literacy assessments do you use? How do these impact how you organize your instruction?
3. *Next*, take this question and create a survey (Survey Monkey and Google both have great surveys—click on the links above to see a tutorial on both of these). Remember, the key to a good survey is to create *good questions*. Use your Inquiry Support Groups to help craft questions. Share your questions and give feedback to one another.
4. *Finally*, send your survey out to teachers at your school. You may want to explain that this is for a class project and that responses will be anonymous and none of this will be shared outside of this course.
5. You need a minimum of *five* respondents.
6. Make sure to give your respondents a date to complete your survey, as you cannot complete Task Two until you get your responses!

Task Two

1. Once you send your respondents the link to your survey, give them about a week to complete this.
2. Both Survey Monkey and Google Forms have features that will help you analyze your data.

3. You will want to share what you learned with your support group. Use this group to help you make sense of this information and also to help you figure out the best way to analyze these data.
4. You do not have to do a statistical analysis, but you should at least describe in detail what your data tell you.
5. Answer the following questions:
   a. How did your findings answer your initial question?
   b. What did you learn about literacy assessment in your school or community?
   c. What does your data say about one of the big issues in literacy assessment?

Task Three

1. Finally, you will submit two final papers on this project: a Reflection and a Final Report.
   a. *Reflection*—The reflection is a 300–500 word reflective essay. This essay will be shared with the whole class through the Class Discussion Board. Students will be required to submit their essay to share with the whole class and then comment on classmates' essays as well. Some questions that should be covered in this essay are:
      • What did you learn through this project about literacy assessment?
      • What did you learn about assessment at your school or community?
      • What would you change about how assessment is conducted in your local environment?
   b. *Final Project Report*—in addition to a reflective essay, students will also submit a brief Final Project Report to the instructor via the Submit Assignments tab. The following sections will be included in this report:
      • Question
      • Survey
      • Data Analysis

ASSIGNMENT 4: THEORETICAL PERSPECTIVES PROJECT

Part One: Perspectives in the Field Demonstrations

The first four components of your project are devoted to historical and current perspectives on reading and writing that fall within the following broad categories: cognitive, linguistic, sociocultural, and motivational. Within each demonstration, describe the following:

- A definition of the broad category (i.e., cognitive, linguistic, sociocultural, or motivational) and a description of the major perspectives (e.g., schema theory, reader response theory, critical theory) that are addressed within this category. Explain/illustrate why you have put them into this category.
- An explanation and illustration of how this category of perspectives addresses students experiencing reading/writing difficulty, including a potential source of difficulty and implications for instruction.
- An example/illustration of how this category of perspectives links to practice. Describe or show an instructional, assessment, or professional development practice that reflects this category of perspectives.
- A historical perspective on this category of perspectives: Where have we been, where are we now, and where are we going as a field with respect to the perspectives within this category?

Part Two: Perspectives in My Professional Life Demonstration

Your final demonstration focuses on your individual, evolving perspectives on the key processes shaping reading and writing and will include the following: your current model or theory of literacy and its connection to theoretical perspectives in the field. This demonstration should address the question of what's happening when someone reads and writes and which theories/models/perspectives are foregrounded in your personal professional perspective.

Your description *must* include your explicit definition of literacy, along with the following elements:

- Its own descriptive name (e.g., the Reading Pyramid; the Solar System of Reading; Reading Is a Train; Gears in Motion: The Multimodal Information Processing Model of Reading)
- The use of visuals or graphics, or other nontextual media, to help explain or illustrate it
- A description/illustration of how your model/theory links to practice. This can be a written or spoken, fully developed, exemplar (i.e., the best example you can come up with rather than just any example) and may be accompanied by other supporting media. What is happening in the classroom that reflects your model? What is the teacher doing? What are

students doing? What materials are available? How are students grouped? Consider the instructional elements most important in bringing your model to practice, and describe them.

Further, it may include an analogy or metaphor to help frame it.

ASSIGNMENT 5: PROFESSIONAL DEVELOPMENT EXPERIENCE

Overview

In this assignment you will create a Professional Development Experience, including a presentation that could be presented in a professional study group, staff meeting, seminar, or workshop for paraprofessionals or teachers to assist these stakeholders in the promotion of literacy.

Goals

The experience should do the following:

- Increase the knowledge base for classroom teachers, paraprofessionals, and/or administrators in the use of curriculum materials
- Increase the knowledge base for classroom teachers, paraprofessionals, and/or administrators in the use of technology-based materials
- Increase the knowledge base for classroom teachers, paraprofessionals, and/or administrators in the use of personal professional development plans
- Reflect an evolving and critical understanding of literacy instruction, demonstrated through multiple sources
- Exhibit leadership skills in professional development as well as an awareness of and ability to describe the characteristics of sound professional development programs
- Be relevant to the context identified
- Include a rationale that is thorough and referenced throughout the presentation
- Include goals that are thoroughly embedded within the activities, rationale, and research presented
- Be designed for participants to be actively engaged in the entire process through decisionmaking, implementation, and reflection in a recursive structure reflective of their assessment of needs

- Model strategies and approaches that can be taken to authentic settings and guide participants in their own quest for learning
- Provide multiple methods and strategies for participant consideration and review and allow participants to reflect upon practices throughout the experience
- Allow multiple opportunities to formally and informally evaluate the process as presented and opportunities to revise or deviate from the presentation as necessary
- Include evaluation that is accurately reflective of the content, goals, and process described
- Include a presentation that is well-organized, visually appealing, and incorporate more than just text or simple graphics to convey messages. References for this assignment can be placed at the end and should be in APA style.

Scoring Guide for Professional Development Experience Assessment

Does Not Meet Course Criteria/IRA Standard (0–1 point)	Moderately Meets Course Criteria/IRA Standard (2–3 points)	Meets or Exceeds Course Criteria/IRA Standard (4–5 points)
Topic Selection, Rationale, and Goals (Standard 6.1)		
Topic is not related to literacy instruction, vague or too broad for the scope of the PD experience or audience identified. Rationale for topic is not provided or insufficient references are provided to establish the relevance; goals are missing or unclear	Topic is focused on a specific aspect of literacy instruction relevant to the context/audience identified for the PD experience; relevant rationale for the purpose of the PD experience/topic selected provided, with appropriate references; goals for the experience are stated and tied into the events surrounding the experience	Topic reflects an evolving and critical understanding of literacy instruction, demonstrated through multiple sources within the presentation and relevant to the context identified; rationale is thorough and referenced throughout the presentation; goals are thoroughly embedded within the activities, rationale, and research presented
Participant Involvement (Standards 6.1, 6.3)		
PD experience is limited; Opportunities for participants to identify issues or goals, and create solutions or processes to work toward goals are missing or cursory; key stakeholders (paraprofessionals, administrators, etc.) are not incorporated into the plans; structure of events is inauthentic or lacks substance	PD experience represents a scaffolded approach to development over time; participants are actively engaged in identifying authentic concerns related to the topic, and then working toward viable solutions within the school context; PD includes components for or recognition of the roles of various stakeholders	PD experience includes modeling, scaffolding, and multiple opportunities over time for participants using authentic and contextually based data; participants are actively engaged in the entire process through decisionmaking, implementation, and reflection in a recursive structure reflective of their assessment of needs within the context as described
PD Educator Involvement (Standards 6.1, 6.2, 6.3)		
PD educator controls the entire experience with little or no input from the participants	PD educator serves as a coach and model for the participants, actively engaging them in the discussion and plan	PD educator serves as an active resource for the participants; guides participants in their own quest for learning; models strategies and approaches in authentic settings; provides multiple methods and strategies for participant consideration and review; participates in reflective practices throughout the experience; displays positive attitudes toward his or her own reading and writing; and models his or her ongoing individual professional development regarding the teaching of reading and writing

Differentiation and Diversity (Standards 6.3, 4.1, 4.2)		
Limited attention to differentiation in the PD experience; limited or no attention to diversity in the knowledge base, strategies, and dispositions addressed	PD experience includes attention to the differentiated knowledge and experiences of participants. PD experience acknowledges PreK–12 student diversity.	PD experience supports learning for participants who range in experiences, dispositions, and knowledge regarding the topic. Methods and strategies of presentation and participant engagement are varied; context of PD experience supports risk-taking and community-building among participants. Knowledge and practical applications support participants in heightening their recognition and understanding of the many forms of diversity in literacy learning; concepts and instructional strategies will positively impact PreK–12 students' engagement with features of diversity

Assessment and Evaluation (Standard 6.3)		
Opportunities for evaluation of the PD experience are cursory or nonexistent; assessment/evaluation opportunities are not accurately reflective of the content, goals, or process as presented in the PD plan	Multiple opportunities for evaluation of the PD experience in both formal and informal ways are provided in the PD plan; assessment/evaluation accurately reflects the content, goals, and process as presented in the PD plan	Evaluation/assessment is embedded within the PD plan; participants are provided multiple opportunities to formally and informally evaluate the process as presented in the plan and opportunities to revise or deviate from the plan as necessary are built into the process as presented; evaluation is accurately reflective of the content, goals, and process described

Professional Role, Presentation, and Style (Standard 6.4)		
PD educator does not model professional leadership with respect to policy decisions and/or does not model professional presentation in content conveyed; multiple typos/grammatical errors; references missing or not in APA format; slides are busy, cluttered, or difficult to read	PD educator addresses the role of instructional leaders as participants in policy conversations. In his or her presentation of content, there are minimal errors; references are present and in APA style; slides are self-sufficient, understandable, and organized in a logical, orderly manner	PD educator models the responsibilities and dispositions of professional leadership, including attention to his or her role, as well as the potential roles of participants in local, state, or national conversations and policy decisions. In presentation of content, PD educator has no errors; APA style is present; references are included; presentation is well-organized, visually appealing, and incorporate more than just text or simple graphics to convey messages

Discussion Rubrics

DISCUSSION RUBRIC 1: THREADED DISCUSSION EXPECTATIONS

Overview

Students are expected to participate fully in threaded discussions (TD, sometimes called Forums) in our course. Such discussions are one of the best pathways for learning, since the experience and thinking of your classmates can further your understanding, and your classmates can learn from you, too!

These discussions require you to carefully read assigned material and then make connections among key ideas and synthesize your learning through thoughtful written responses. There are three things that we are looking for when we grade your engagement in threaded discussions. First, we look for a *substantive initial post* about the material. This is your initial contribution to the discussion and should be able to keep the discussion going. Then we want you to be really engaged in at least *one other student's posts* with a *substantive response*—basically, you are engaging in a conversation with these students and offering new ideas or thoughts to this discussion. However, we also realize that when you participate in good discussions there is room for comments such as "good idea" and "I like your thinking" (this is like nodding your head in a real discussion). We want to know you are reading and thinking about this discussion and want you to acknowledge this through at least *3–4 other supportive posts*, which do not have to be as lengthy.

Sample Holistic Grading Scale

3 (Exceeds)	2 (Meets)	1 (Done)
Substantive Initial Post		
Initial post is *substantive* where students integrate the reading for the week with their professional experiences and include specific examples and/or substantiating evidence to support their responses. Initial post is entered early in the week (by Wednesday) to enable others to interact with the post. Initial post stimulates a deep discussion about the material. Initial post reflects high standards of graduate student work and thoughtful effort about the material.	Initial post integrates the reading for the week with their professional experiences and/or includes specific examples and/or substantiating evidence to support his or her response. Initial post is entered (by Friday) to enable others to interact with the post. Initial post stimulates a discussion about the material. Initial post reflects graduate student work and thoughtful effort about the material.	Initial post integrates the reading for the week with their professional experiences and includes specific examples and/or substantiating evidence to support his or her response. Initial post is completed (by Saturday). Initial post connects to the material.
Engaged Dialogue		
Student makes a thoughtful and engaged response to *more than one* classmate. This response includes giving additional information, probing a topic further, sharing a new example, or asking a further question. This response continues the conversation and invites others to think deeply about this topic.	Student makes a thoughtful and engaged response to *one* classmate. This response includes giving additional information, probing a topic further, sharing a new example, or asking a further question.	Student does not make a thoughtful response.
Supportive Dialogue		
Student makes four supportive comments on classmates' threads that demonstrate that he or she is reading and engaging with other people's posts on a topic. Supportive dialogue can include things like "Good point" and "Have you thought about . . ."	Student makes 2–3 supportive comments on classmates' threads that demonstrate that he or she is reading and engaging with others' posts on a topic.	Student makes one supportive comment on classmates' threads that demonstrate that he or she is reading and engaging with others' posts on a topic.

Annotated Exemplar of Discussion

Substantive Initial Post

Routman (2005) says that writing instruction should be
a whole-part-whole idea. She really goes against teaching skills in isolation. "I have not been able to locate any
research showing that worksheets or drills carry over
into students' successful application of skills in authentic
reading/writing contexts" (p. 142). This seems to be the
biggest conversation among teachers in our school. Students are good at finding mistakes in my writing or sample
writing, but they don't find it in their own writing. Routman also says, "Skills instruction should intrude as little
as possible upon students' ongoing efforts at constructing
meaning from text" (p. 143). In my classroom I will be
honest, I'm in flux. . . . I want to give my students as much
time to write as possible (our 2-hour block for language
arts gives about 30–35 minutes of writing time) but then I
have to justify why students don't do as well as others on
writing tests, and so I revert to the old drills to "help." My
administration and district want to see mini lessons almost
daily, the district set out our pacing guide with the state
standards in mind and limits what we can "write" to descriptive and narrative. Our school echoes that and doesn't
want see anything else. My principal is very test oriented
and so our need to show students how to take the state
writing test and the multiple choice portion of the test that
deals with identifying complete sentences and how to read
the answer choices and questions to help them understand
is pressured on us daily. I am hoping that I can learn ways
to improve my instruction that fits my beliefs that the students need to have more choice in what they are writing,
but also fill the expectations set forth from the district and
my administration.

Connect to text

Connect to real experience

Connect to text

Gives opinion

Goal

Engaged Dialogue

I was talking about this exact thing with another 3rd-grade
teacher and a 4th-grade teacher, and I think a lot of those
things are exactly what I'm going to do. I want to make
sure that I'm giving them some options for writing ideas. I
think right now I do a good job of letting them share their
writing; on Fridays we do a "milling to music" where they

Connection to previous post

Sharing personal experience

take their free write journals and they walk around and until the music stops and then share something they've written with the person they are next to. I am also going to focus on doing mini lessons in smaller groups, and in the middle of class instead of always at the beginning. I'm hoping that by giving them a chance to write before we talk about what we're writing will help them see the whole piece instead of the smaller parts.

Action

Supportive Dialogue

Building on idea— positive reinforcement

GREAT sharing idea! I teach older kids but have one class that is really boisterous and kinesthetic. They love to talk to each other and have trouble sitting still, especially for an 85-minute block class. This is a great idea to get them up and moving and talking about their writing! Thanks. ←──── **Supportive**

DISCUSSION RUBRIC 2: RUBRIC FOR DISCUSSION BOARD CONVERSATIONS ABOUT THEORIES OF READING

Standard	Standard Is Met or Exceeded 2 points	Standard Is Partially Met 1.5 points	Standard Is Not Met 0–1 point
Candidate has read the material carefully and not superficially. (For Monday posts, "the material" refers to class readings. For Thursday posts, "the material" refers to the post you are replying to as well as class readings.)	Strong evidence of careful, critical thinking	Moderate evidence of careful, critical thinking	Weak or no evidence of careful, critical thinking
Candidate addresses the prompt when a prompt is given	Prompt is clearly addressed in post	Post is partially connected to prompt	Lack of clear connection between prompt and post
Candidate is proactive in understanding complex material	Strong evidence of comments and questions aimed and clarifying concepts or elaborating on understanding	Moderate evidence of comments and questions aimed and clarifying concepts or elaborating on understanding	Weak evidence of comments and questions aimed and clarifying concepts or elaborating on understanding
Candidate meets criteria for number and length of posts in forum	Meets or exceeds required number of posts and length approximations	Meets required number of posts and length approximations	Does not meet required number of posts and/or length approximations
Professional demeanor and disposition	Consistently meets or exceeds expectation for professional, respectful communication	Usually meets expectation for professional, respectful communication	Does not regularly meet the expectation for professional, respectful communication

Sample Professional Development Grid

Woodstock Vocabulary PLC: 2012–13
Facilitator: Carolyn Gwinn
Professional Development Grid

Record of Vocabulary Instruction, Student Learning, and Teacher Reflections

Please complete the grid on the following page each month and submit it to Carolyn prior to each PLC meeting. Please send it as an email attachment.

Name: Chris
Month: February
Grade/Role: Grade 4 Humanities Teacher

Student Learning Objectives	Vocabulary Approach/ Instructional Practice Potential Link to Resource (e.g., colleague, text, curriculum, own investigation)	Evidence of Learning: To what degree have student objectives been met?	Work Sample	Future Instructional Plans	Teacher Reflections
The learning objective was to learn 4 of the most commonly used prefixes (un-, re-, in-, dis-) and some commonly used suffixes (-ful, -less, -ness)	Thinking about Michael Graves's Chapter 5: Teaching Word Learning Strategies, I decided to focus on prefix and suffix work. Using word parts to figure out words is a close second to using context clues. During this time, the students had homework where they had to come up with words that had the prefixes and suffixes we were learning. We discussed how there had to be a root word in order for it to be considered an actual prefix. We added words to our prefix/suffix wall.	I gave a prefix, root word, suffix assessment. There were 4 parts. Part 1: They had to tell what each prefix and suffix meant. Part 2: There were 14 words. They had to circle the words that had prefixes and cross out the words that did not. Part 3: They had to come up with a word using each prefix and suffix. They then had to tell what each word meant. Part 4: I gave them 3 words and they had to take each word apart. (ex: unhappiness, un+happy+ness) This assessment gave me a lot of information. Part 1 told me if they knew what each prefix and suffix meant. Part 2 told me if they knew that in order to be considered a prefix, you needed to have a base/root word when you took away the prefix. Part 3 told me if they could come up with an actual word that had the prefix or suffix and what it means. Part 4 told me if they could break apart words into the different parts (prefix, root, suffix).	The assessment could be a work sample. The homework sheet could also be a work sample.	I would like to continue to add to our list of prefixes and suffixes, especially suffixes that we are learning.	I was very pleased with how the students did on the assessment. 51 students averaged 90% on the assessment. They are beginning to realize how many words they come across in their own reading have prefixes and suffixes we've been learning. They are definitely more aware and understand how this can help them learn new words. I can now use the results to form intervention groups based on the needs of individual students.

References

Allen, I. E., Seaman, J., & Garrett, R. (2007). *Blending in: The extent and promise of blended education in the United States.* Newburyport, MA: The Sloan Consortium.

Allington, R. L., & Johnston, P. (2002). *Reading to learn: Lessons from exemplary fourth-grade classrooms.* New York, NY: Guilford.

American Association of Colleges for Teacher Education. (2011). *Transformations in educator preparation: Effectiveness and accountability.* Washington, DC: American Association of Colleges for Teacher Education.

Amiel, T., & Reeves, T. C. (2008). Design-based research and educational technology: Rethinking technology and the research agenda. *Educational Technology & Society, 11,* 29–40.

Amory, A. (2012). Tool-mediated authentic learning in an educational technology course: A designed-based innovation. *Interactive Learning Environments,* 1–17, DOI:10.1080/10494820.2012.682584

An, Y., & Reigeluth, C. M. (2008). Problem-based learning in online environments. *The Quarterly Review of Distance Education, 9*(1), 1–16.

Ash, K. (2012).Common core raises PD opportunities, questions. *Education Week, 2*(5), 4–5. Retrieved from http://www.edweek.org/tsb/articles/2012/03/01/02common.h05.html

Aspden, L., & Helm, P. (2004). Making the connection in a blended learning environment. *Educational Media International, 41*(3), 245–252.

Barab, S., Schatz, S., & Scheckler, R. (2004). Using activity theory to conceptualize online community and using online community to conceptualize activity theory. *Mind, Culture, and Activity, 11*(1), 25–47.

Baran, E., Correia, A., & Thompson, A. (2011). Transforming online teaching practice: Critical analysis of the literature on the roles and competencies of online teachers. *Distance Education, 32*(3), 421–439.

Bennett, S., & Lockyer, L. (2004). Becoming an online teacher: Adapting to a changed environment for teaching and learning in higher education. *Educational Media International, 41*(3), 231–244.

Berk, R. (2009). Multimedia teaching with video clips: TV, movies, YouTube, and mtvU in the college classroom. *International Journal of Technology in Teaching and Learning, 5*(1), 1–21.

Bloom, B. S. (1956). *Taxonomy of educational objectives, handbook I: The cognitive domain.* New York, NY: David McKay.

Borko, H., Whitcomb, J., & Liston, D. (2009). Wicked problems and other thoughts on issues of technology and teacher learning. *Journal of Teacher Education, 60*(1), 3–7.

Brown, R. E. (2001). The process of community building in distance learning classes. *Asynchronous Learning Networks, 5*(2), 18–35.

Caulfield, J. (2011). *How to design and teach a hybrid course: Achieving student-centered learning through blended classroom, online, and experiential activities.* Sterling, VA: Stylus Publishing.

Chandler-Olcott, K., & Lewis, E. (2010). Screen and scrapbooking: Sociocultural perspectives on new literacies. In E. A. Baker (Ed.), *The new literacies: Multiple perspectives on research and practice* (pp. 194–216). New York, NY: Guilford.

Chickering, A. W., & Gamson, Z. F. (1987). Seven principles for good practice in undergraduate education. *AAHE Bulletin, 39*(1), 3–7.

Churches, A. (2009). *Bloom's digital taxonomy.* Retrieved from http://edorigami.wikispaces.com/Bloom's+Digital+Taxonomy

Clarke, L. W. (2012). Putting asynchronous discussions under the lens: Improving discussions through student examination. *Distance Learning, 9*(3), 43–50.

Coiro, J., Knobel, M., Lankshear, C., & Leu, D. J. (2009). Central issues in new literacies and new literacies research. In J. Coiro, M. Knobel, C. Lankshear, & D. J. Leu (Eds.), *Handbook of research on new literacies* (pp. 1–21). New York, NY: Routledge.

Council of Chief State School Officers. (2011). *Interstate Teacher Assessment and Support Consortium (InTASC) model core teaching standards: A resource for state dialogue.* Washington, DC: Author.

Darling-Hammond, L. (2006). *Powerful teacher education: Lessons from exemplary programs.* San Francisco, CA: Jossey-Bass.

Darling-Hammond, L., Wei, R. C., Andree, A., Richardson, N., & Orphanos, S. (2009). *Professional learning in the learning profession: A status report on teacher development in the United States and abroad.* Dallas, TX: National Staff Development Council.

de Bono, E. (1985). *Six thinking hats: An essential approach to business management.* New York, NY: Little, Brown, & Company.

Dennis, D. V. (2009). "I'm not stupid": How assessment drives (in)appropriate reading instruction. *Journal Of Adolescent & Adult Literacy, 53*(4), 283–290.

Dewey, J. (1916). *Democracy and education: An introduction to the philosophy of education.* New York, NY: Free Press.

Diekelmann, N., Schuster, R., & Nosek, C. (1998). *Creating new pedagogies at the millennium: The common experience of the University of Wisconsin–Madison teachers using distance education technologies.* Retrieved from http://www.uwsa.edu/ttt/articles/98.pdf

DuFour, R., DuFour, R., Eaker, R., & Many, T. (2010). *Learning by doing: A handbook for professional learning communities at work* (2nd ed.). Bloomington, IN: Solution Tree.

Dunne, F., Nave, B., & Lewis, A. (2000). Critical friends groups: Teachers helping teachers to improve student learning. *Phi Delta Kappan, 28,* 9–12.

Edwards, M., Perry, B., & Janzen, K. (2011). The making of an exemplary online educator. *Distance Education, 32*(1), 101–118.

Ferguson, R. (1991). Paying for public education: New evidence on how and why money matters. *Harvard Journal on Legislation, 28,* 465–498.

Gambrell, L. B., Malloy, J. A., & Mazzoni, S. A. (2011). Evidence-based best practice in comprehensive literacy instruction. In L. M. Morrow & L. B. Gambrell (Eds.), *Best practices in literacy instruction* (4th ed., pp. 11–36). New York, NY: Guilford.

Garrison, D. R., Anderson, T., & Archer, W. (2000). Critical inquiry in a text-based environment: Computer conferencing in higher education. *The Internet and Higher Education, 2*(2–3), 1–19.

Garrison, D. R., & Vaughn, N. (2008). *Blended learning in higher education: Framework, principles, and guidelines.* San Francisco: Jossey-Bass.

Gwinn, C. B., & Watts-Taffe, S. (2013, April). *The power of comprehensive vocabulary instruction to boost student learning and help meet the English language arts common core standards: One elementary school's story.* Paper presented at the annual conference of the International Reading Association, San Antonio, TX.

Haggerty, N., Schneberger, S., & Carr, P. (2001). Exploring media influences on individual learning: Implications for organizational learning. In J. DeGross, S. Sarkar, & V. Storey (Eds.), *Proceedings, International Conference on Information Systems* (pp. 13–22). New Orleans, LA: Association for Information Systems.

Henning, W. (2004). Everyday cognition and situated learning. In D. Jonassen (Ed.), *Handbook of research on educational communications and technology* (2nd ed., pp. 143–168). Mahwah, NJ: Lawrence Erlbaum.

Hsu, S. (2004). Using case discussion on the web to develop student teacher problem solving skills. *Teaching and Teacher Education: An International Journal of Research and Studies, 20*(7), 681–692.

International Reading Association/National Council of Teachers of English. (1996). *Standards for the English language arts.* Newark, DE: Author.

International Reading Association. (2009). *Position statement on new literacies and 21st century technologies.* Newark, DE: Author.

International Reading Association. (2010). *Standards for reading professionals (Revised 2010).* Newark, DE: Author.

International Society for Technology in Education. (2012). *ISTE standards.* Washington, DC: Author. Retrieved from www.iste.org/standards/

Johnson, L. L. (2012, December). *Experience of the online learner.* Paper presented at the annual meeting of the Literacy Research Association, San Diego, CA.

Johnston, P., & Costello, P. (2005). Theory and research into practice: Principles for literacy assessment. *Reading Research Quarterly, 40*(2), 256–267.

Kaleta, R., Skibba, K. A., & Joosten, T. (2007). Discovering, designing, and delivering hybrid courses. In A. Picciano & C. Dziuban (Eds.), *Blended learning: Research perspectives* (pp. 111-143). Needham, MA: The Sloan Consortium.

Karchmer, R. A., Mallette, M. H., Kara-Soteriou, J., & Leu, D. J. (2005). *Innovative approaches to literacy education: Using the Internet to support new literacies.* Newark, DE: International Reading Association.

Lave, J., & Wenger, E. (1991). *Situated learning: Legitimate peripheral participation.* Cambridge, UK: Cambridge University Press.

Leander, K. (2012, November). *Integrative research review: Designing new spaces for literacy learning.* Paper presented at the annual meeting of the Literacy Research Association, San Diego, CA.

Lee, K. S. (2009). Listening to students: Investigating the effectiveness of an on-line graduate teaching strategy course. *Journal of Online Learning and Teaching, 51*(1), 72–87.

Levin, A. (2006). Educating school teachers. *The Education Schools Project.* Retrieved from http://www.edschools.org/pdf/Educating_Teachers_Report.pdf

Leu, D. J. (2007, May). *What happened when we weren't looking? How reading comprehension has changed and what we need to do about it.* Keynote address presented at the annual convention of the International Reading Association's Reading Research Conference, Toronto, Canada.

Leu, D. J., Kinzer, C. G., Coiro, J., & Cammack, D. (2004). Toward a theory of new literacies emerging from the Internet and other information and communication technologies. In R. R. Ruddell & N. J. Unrauh (Eds.), *Theoretical models and processes of reading* (5th ed., pp. 1570–1613). Newark, DE: International Reading Association.

Major, C. H. (2010). Do virtual professors dream of electric students? University faculty experiences with online distance education. *Teachers College Record, 112*(8), 2154–2208.

Marsh, J. P., Lammers, J. C., & Alvermann, D. (2012). Quality assurance in online content literacy methods courses. *Literacy Research and Instruction, 51,* 233–253.

McCarthey, S. J., & Moje, E. B. (2002). Identity matters. *Reading Research Quarterly, 37,* 228–237.

McDonald, J. P., Zydney, J. M., Dichter, A., & McDonald, E. C. (2012). *Going online with protocols: New tools for teaching and learning.* New York, NY: Teachers College Press.

McKenna, M. C., & Walpole, S. (2005). Assessment: How well does assessment inform our reading instruction? *Reading Teacher, 59*(1), 84–86.

McKenzie, B., Mims, N., Bennett, E., & Waugh, M. (2000). Needs, concerns, and practices of online instructors. *Online Journal of Distance Learning Administration, 3*(3). Retrieved from http://www.westga.edu/~distance/ojdla/fall33/mckenzie33.html

Miller, M. V. (2011). A system for integrating online multimedia into college curriculum. *Journal of Online Learning and Teaching, 7*(2). Retrieved from http://jolt.merlot.org/vol7no2/miller_0611.htm

Mohan, L., Lundeberg, M. A., & Reffitt, K. (2008). Studying teachers and schools: Michael Pressley's legacy and directions for future research. *Educational Psychologist, 43*(2), 107–118.

Moll, L., Amanti, C., Neff, D., & Gonzalez, N. (1992). Funds of knowledge for teaching: Using a qualitative approach to connect homes and classrooms. *Theory into Practice, 31,* 132–141.

Moore, M. G., & Kearsley, G. (2012). *Distance education: A systems view of online learning* (3rd ed.). Belmont, CA: Wadsworth.

National Center for Education Statistics. (2000). *Teachers' tools for the 21st century: A report on teachers' use of technology.* Washington, DC: U.S. Department of Education.

National Commission on Teaching and America's Future. (1996, September). *What matters most: Teaching for America's future.* Retrieved from www.teachingpoint.net/Exhibit%20A/What%20Matters%20Most.pdf

National Council for Accreditation of Teacher Education. (2010). *Transforming teacher education through clinical practice: A national strategy to prepare effective educators*. Washington, DC: Author.

National Education Association. (2002). *Guide to teaching online courses*. Washington, DC: NEA. Retrieved from www.nea.org/home/30113.htm

National Governors Association Center for Best Practices & Council of Chief State School Officers. (2010). *Common Core State Standards*. Washington, DC: Authors.

National Institute of Child Health and Human Development. (2000). *Report of the National Reading Panel. Teaching children to read: An evidence-based assessment of the scientific research literature on reading and its implications for reading instruction* (NIH Publication No. 00-4769). Washington, DC: U.S. Government Printing Office.

No Child Left Behind (NCLB) Act of 2001, Pub. L. No. 107-110, § 115, Stat. 1425 (2002).

Outing, S., & Ruel, L. (2004). *The best of eyetrack III: What we saw when we looked through their eyes*. Retrieved from http://www.poynterextra.org/EYETRACK2004/main.htm

Palloff, R., & Pratt, K. (2007). *Building online learning communities*. San Francisco, CA: Jossey-Bass.

Palmer, P. (1998). *The courage to teach: Exploring the inner landscape of a teacher's life*. San Francisco, CA: Jossey-Bass.

Peterson, D. S. (2013). Professional learning: Professional learning communities, whole-school meetings, and cross-school sharing. In B. M. Taylor & N. K. Duke (Eds.), *Handbook of effective literacy instruction* (pp. 530–554). New York, NY: Guilford.

Picciano, A. G. (2007). Introduction. In A. G. Picciano & C. D. Dziuban (Eds.), *Blended learning: Research perspectives* (pp. 5–17). Needham, MA: Sloan Center for Online Education.

Prensky, M. (2001). Digital native's digital immigrants. *On the Horizon, 9*(5), 1–7.

Pressley, M. (2002). *Reading instruction that works*. New York, NY: Guilford Press.

Pressley, M., Wharton-McDonald, R., Hampson, J. M., & Echevarria, M. (1998). The nature of literacy instruction in ten grade-4/5 classrooms in upstate New York. *Scientific Studies of Reading, 2*, 159–191.

Richardson, W. (2010). *Blogs, wikis, podcasts and other powerful web tools for classrooms* (3rd ed.). Thousand Oaks, CA: Corwin Press.

Richardson, J. C., & Swan, K. (2003). Examining social presence in online courses in relation to students' perceived learning and satisfaction. *Journal of Asynchronous Learning Networks, 7*(1).

Rideout, V. J., Foehr, U. G., & Roberts, D. F. (2010). *Generation M2: Media in the lives of 8- to 18-year-olds*. Menlo Park, CA: The Henry J. Kaiser Family Foundation.

Risko, V. J., & Walker-Dalhouse, D. (2010). Making the most of assessments to inform instruction. *Reading Teacher, 63*(5), 420–422.

Roblyer, M. D., Porter, M., Bielefeldt, T., & Donaldson, M. (2009). "Teaching online made me a better teacher": Studying the impact of virtual course experiences on teachers' face-to-face practice. *Journal of Computing in Teacher Education, 25*(4), 121–126.

Routman, R. (2005). *Writing essentials: Raising expectations and results while simplifying teaching*. Portsmouth, NH: Heinemann.

Rovai, A. P. (2004). A constructivist approach to online college learning. *The Internet and Higher Education, 7,* 79–93.

Rovai, A. P. (2007). Facilitating online discussions effectively. *Internet and Higher Education, 10*(1), 77–88.

Saltmarsh, S., & Sutherland-Smith, W. (2010). S(t)imulating learning: Pedagogy, subjectivity and teacher education in online environments. *London Review of Education, 8*(1), 15–24.

Shea, P., Fredericksen, E., Pickett, A., & Pelz, W. (2004). Faculty development, student satisfaction, and reported learning in the SUNY learning network. In T. Duffy & J. Kirkley (Eds.), *Learner-centered theory and practice in distance education* (p. 343–377). Mahwah, NJ: Lawrence Erlbaum.

Sherer, P. D., Shea, T. P., & Kristensen, E. (2003). Online communities of practice: A catalyst for faculty development. *Innovative Higher Education, 27,* 183–194.

Sheridan, K., & Kelly, M. A. (2010). The indicators of instructor presence that are important to students in online courses. *MERLOT Journal of Online Teaching and Learning, 6*(4),767–779.

Silvers, P., O'Conneell, J., Fewell, M. (2007). Strategies for creating community in a graduate education online program. *Journal of Computing in Teacher Education, 23*(3), 81–87.

Smith, T. C. (2005). Fifty-one competencies for online instruction. *The Journal of Educators Online, 2*(2), 2–18.

Sloan Consortium (2011). *Going the distance: Online education in the United States, 2011.* Retrieved from http://sloanconsortium.org/publications/survey/going_distance_2011

Stacey, E., & Gerbic, P. (2008, December). *Success factors for blended learning.* Paper presented at the annual conference of the Australasian Society for Computers in Learning in Tertiary Education, Melbourne, Australia.

Swan, K., & Shea, P. (2005). The development of virtual learning communities. In S. Hiltz & R. Goldman (Eds.), *Learning together online: Research on asynchronous learning networks* (pp. 239–260). Mahwah, NJ: Lawrence Erlbaum.

Tatum, A. W. (2011). Diversity and literacy. In S. J. Samuels & A. E. Farstrup (Eds.), *What research has to say about reading instruction* (4th ed., 425–447). Newark, DE: International Reading Association.

Taylor, B. M. (2011). *Catching schools.* Portsmouth, NH: Heinemann.

Topping, K., & Ferguson, N. (2005). Effective literacy teaching behaviors. *Journal of Research in Reading, 28*(2), 125–143.

Toppo, G., & Schnaars, C. (2012, August 8). Online education degrees skyrocket. *USA Today.* Retrieved from http://www.usatoday.com/news/education/story/2012-08-07/online-teaching-degrees/56849026/1

Trevitt, C., & Perera, C. (2009). Self and continuing professional learning (development): Issues of curriculum and identity in developing academic practice. *Teaching in Higher Education, 14*(4), 347–359.

U.S. Department of Education. (2009). *Race to the Top program: Executive summary.* Retrieved from www2.ed.gov/programs/racetothetop/executive-summary.pdf

U.S. Department of Education. (2011). *Our future, our teachers: The Obama administration's plan for teacher education reform and improvement.* Retrieved from www.ed.gov/sites/default/files/our-future-our-teachers.pdf

Vignare, K. (2007). Review of literature: Blended learning: Using ALN to change the classroom—Will it work? In A. G. Picciano & C. D. Dziuban (Eds.), *Blended learning: Research perspectives* (pp. 37–63). Needham, MA: Sloan Center for Online Education.

Vygotsky, L. S. (1962). *Thought and language*. Cambridge, MA: MIT Press.

Vygotsky, L. S. (1978). *Mind in society: The development of higher psychological processes*. Cambridge, MA: Harvard University Press.

Wang, Y., & Chen, V. D. T. (2008). Essential elements in designing online discussions to promote cognitive prescience—A practical guide. *Journal of Asynchronous Learning Networks, 12*(3–4), 157–177.

Warschauer, M. (2006). *Laptops and literacy: Learning in the wireless classroom*. New York, NY: Teachers College Press.

Watts-Taffe, S., & Gwinn, C. B. (2007). *Integrating literacy and technology: Effective practice for grades K-6*. New York, NY: Guilford.

Wenger, E. (1998). *Communities of practice: Learning, meaning, and identity*. Cambridge, UK: Cambridge University Press.

Whitesel, C. (1998). *Reframing our classrooms, reframing ourselves: Perspectives from a virtual paladin*. Retrieved from http://technologysource.org/article/reframing_our_classrooms_reframing_ourselves/

Williams, J. A., Rose, C., & Heineke, S. (2012, December). *Change over time: A comparison of online and face-to-face discussions over two semesters*. Paper presented at annual Literacy Research Association Conference, San Diego, CA.

Wray, D., Medwell, J., Fox, R., Poulson, L. (2000). The teaching practices of effective teachers of literacy. *Educational Review, 52*(1), 75–84.

Young, S. (2006). Student views of effective online teaching in higher education. *The American Journal of Distance Education, 20*(2), 65–77.

Young, S., & Shaw, D. G. (1999). Profiles of effective college and university teachers. *The Journal of Higher Education, 70*(6), 670–686.

Index

A page number followed by an *f* indicates a figure.

About the Authors

Lane W. Clarke, EdD, is the literacy concentration leader for the online master's in science of education at the University of New England. She enjoys working with graduate students in an online format and is always pushing herself and others to explore innovative pedagogy to increase the effectiveness of online teaching and learning. In addition to teaching online, Lane also teaches undergraduate pre-service teachers in literacy pedagogy. She has published two other books, *High Tech Teaching Success* (Prufrock Press, 2009, with Kevin Besnoy) and *The Reading Turn Around* (Teachers College Press, 2009, with Stephanie Jones and Grace Enriquez), as well as articles in journals such as *The Reading Teacher, Language Arts, Journal of Adolescent and Adult Literacy, Journal of Literacy Research, Journal of Media Literacy,* and *Kentucky Reading Journal.* Her research interests include literacy education, online teaching and learning, reading comprehension, literacy and technology, and classroom discourse. In her rare free time she loves to read (not surprisingly) and spend time with her family enjoying the outdoors in Maine.

Susan Watts-Taffe, PhD, is an associate professor of literacy education at the University of Cincinnati, where she teaches undergraduate and graduate courses and coordinates professional development opportunities for teachers in the region. She regularly teaches online courses in the University's Reading Endorsement program, which was launched under her direction. She has served on several national committees, including the International Reading Association's RTI Commission, and her articles appear in journals such as *Reading Research Quarterly, The Reading Teacher,* and *Journal of Adolescent and Adult Literacy.* She is co-author (with Camille Blachowicz, Peter Fisher, and Donna Ogle) of *Teaching Academic Vocabulary K–8: Effective Practice Across the Curriculum* (Guilford Press, 2013) and (with Carolyn B. Gwinn) *Integrating Literacy and Technology: Effective Practice in Grades K–6* (Guilford Press, 2007). Her research interests include literacy-technology integration, vocabulary instruction, and teacher professional development. In her spare time, she enjoys spending time with her two children and her husband in Cincinnati, Ohio.